HUNGRY

WHAT EIGHTY RAVENOUS GUYS TAUGHT ME ABOUT LIFE, LOVE, AND THE POWER OF GOOD FOOD

HUN

DARLENE BARNES

GRY

ΑΣΦ

HYPERION

NEW YORK

Grateful acknowledgment is made to the following for permission to reproduce illustrations: pages ii–iii (title page spread), photograph courtesy of John Richmond/John Richmond Photography (www.johnrichmondphotography .com); page 104, photograph courtesy of Ronald Johnson; page 153, photograph courtesy of Darlene Barnes.

Library of Congress Cataloging-in-Publication Data

Barnes, Darlene.
  Hungry/Darlene Barnes.—First edition.
    pages cm.
  ISBN 978-1-4013-2477-3
  1. Barnes, Darlene.   2. Women cooks—Washington (State)—Seattle—Biography.   3. Cooks—Washington (State)—Seattle—Biography.
4. Cooking—Washington (State)—Seattle—Psychological aspects.
5. Food—Washington (State)—Seattle—Psychological aspects.   6. Greek letter societies—Washington (State)—Seattle.   7. Male college students—Washington (State)—Seattle—Social life and customs.   8. Male college students—Washington (State)—Seattle—Psychology.   9. Middle-aged women—Washington (State)—Seattle—Biography.   I. Title.
  TX649.B37A3 2013
  641.5092—dc23

                                                              2012047322

Design by Renato Stanisic

FIRST EDITION

10   9   8   7   6   5   4   3   2   1

SUSTAINABLE FORESTRY INITIATIVE   Certified Sourcing   www.sfiprogram.org   SFI-00993

THIS LABEL APPLIES TO TEXT STOCK

TO MY GUYS

CONTENTS

Contents

HUNGRY

How lucky I am to have something that makes saying goodbye so hard.

—A. A. MILNE, *WINNIE-THE-POOH*

INTRODUCTION

Is it what you expected?" one of my guys asked me several years into the role of cooking for the men of Alpha Sigma Phi on the University of Washington campus. I paused a long time, thinking back to the job ad and the interview, before answering that I was surprised by how unexpected it had turned out to be. I had taken the job with very limited knowledge of this secretive culture, thinking that I would challenge the notion of "frat food" as nothing more than pizza and fries. But I had not realized how many other challenges lay ahead, and how they were not all about food, and that a paycheck was the least of the rewards.

Several years before starting the job, my older son, Sean, was a freshman in college when he called with the surprising announcement that he'd joined a fraternity, the first person I was related to who had ever done so. He'd left home for New York State and we were in Texas, where Sean had graduated in the top 10 percent of his high school class, played clarinet in the band, and was generally a quiet, gentle kid. He was fully prepared academically, but he was somewhat isolated in his dorm room far from home until someone from the fraternity came by to invite him into their world. My husband, Phil, would later observe that what Sean had gained most from his college years wasn't the computer science degree; it was the life lessons in "beer and friendship." So when I took the job cooking for the men of Alpha Sigma Phi, the few concrete images in my head weren't of hazing and raucous parties; they were of community and belonging.

I'd stayed home most of the years that Sean and his younger brother, Simon, lived at home. But I had taken various jobs—food related and otherwise—while he was in high school and was a private chef to a Dallas billionaire just before we moved to Seattle, where Phil had accepted a position with Microsoft. I followed him a few months later, without a job myself, but I was determined to find some occupation other than having manicures at the Pro Club and shopping at Nordstrom; at forty-two, with two sons now on their own, I was determined to create something of *my* own.

But frat cook had not been the plan. "That's a job?" people would ask me, and I admit that it's a question I asked myself several months into it. When Sean told me about Greek system cooks a few years before I became one, I had thought it a puzzling occupation, like circus clown or spy. It was something I knew people did but that I would never do; the idea of working in a fraternity seemed as foreign to me as actually pledging one. So it is a perplexing thing to find myself still in the same kitchen six years later when I had not actively sought this out and when I had never stayed with any other job for a third of that time. It's a dirty place and a physically draining job and almost no one anywhere, let alone in the food business, takes you seriously when they learn where you work. It is not respected or glamorous or a boost to a résumé. And I can't seem to leave, though I have tried.

When I set out to write a book about this experience, I was clear about what it was not going to be: It would not be a manual on sustainable cooking in a frat house, or a listing of recipes. And it wouldn't be a trotting out of all the old clichés about fraternities, a rehash (or a defense for that matter) of isolated negative news stories, or an exposé of the secret rituals, which, as I often had to reassure the guys' alumni adviser, no one on the "outside" cares about anyway. "Even we don't care," one of the guys quipped when he asked me what the book would be. And while I wanted it to be funny, I didn't want it to be a joke.

I had expected it to be a story about physical and emotional hunger of young men at a critical turning point in their lives, but what I hadn't realized until I was nearly finished was how much my own quite different life experiences mirrored their fundamental struggles and how a thread of being the outsider wanting in runs through it all. I was struck that while I worked in a heavily male-dominated profession in an all-male workplace, and suffered a fair amount of condescension from many of those males outside the House, I felt empowered, respected, and valued by the people in this quintessential boys' club. I thought I was there not just to feed them, but to teach them, and was surprised to find out how much I didn't know, how wrong I often was, how quick I was to judge, and how the hunger was not all on their side. And I wanted to write about it because it seemed to me that the longing for connection and purpose, not to mention a heavy dose of laughter and fun in life, was a longing that was not mine alone.

Pelling

Ford

We love You

you for everything
you the best
Thanks Osegena
for the good food
Jeffey

Thanks for everything

Matt H.

I love your food
-John Z

Thanks Darlene

♥ Alex N

Alex
Vg

Derek
V

Seth
Tai

Jall

Ari De

Charlie
Redann

Alex
Walker

The Best!
Thank you
Darlene?
Mike Hunlay

James Leask

for hard

Thanks Darlene!
-Blair

Darlene, Av

Patrick

Darlene,
Thank you!
Daniel Stoecker

Stuart Reeden
Steve Hang

you for
hing Shane
For all that you do.
Happy New Year!
Nick D.

hungry

Chp

Richard Weyrich
Your boys of,
Alpha Sigma P

U
Michael Marte

1

Outsider

And your husband is okay with that?" an acquaintance asked when I shared the news that I'd accepted a job cooking for the Alpha Sigma Phi Fraternity on the University of Washington campus in Seattle. From the sultry way she curved her lips around those words, I supposed that she had missed the word "cooking" and I often thought about this when one of the guys would ask me to partner up for beer pong and I would refuse yet again. *Obviously.* Maybe she had thought I'd be all for that. Or maybe she was one of *those* kinds of fortysomething women and supposed I was, too. I had misgivings about working in a frat house, surrounded all day by guys half my age, but it wasn't the prospect of being hit on that scared me; it was the fear that they wouldn't like me at all. Still, I accepted the job believing I had a special understanding about men, having had brothers and sons and more male friends than female, when really I had no clue what was about to hit me. The only thing about my past experience that helped me at all was the knowledge that you have to pick your battles wisely and make good on your threats.

My husband and I had moved to Seattle the summer before I started at the Alpha Sig House, although that wasn't the job that brought us there. Phil had been recruited by a former boss to work at Microsoft headquarters on a new project requiring a hardware engineer, an offer that came just one day after I'd been sitting glumly in our four-thousand-square-foot home in Plano, Texas, asking him, like a sullen child, if I was going to have to live in that house forever where it took me eight hours to clean, vacuum, and weed. I'm sure it was some woman's dream life—all the home improvement TV shows and real estate brochures said so—but it wasn't mine.

Because Phil had moved out months ahead of me, I was left to sell or donate what we couldn't take, which was a lot since we planned to trade our palatial surroundings for an apartment smack in the middle of our new city. And because I couldn't stand the idea of sticking our cats in crates and flying them halfway across the country, my mom accompanied Tess and Emma and me on a road trip that took us through Texas, New Mexico, Colorado, Wyoming, Montana, and Idaho before we reached the Washington border. I'd moved many times and there was always a period when I felt like a visitor, but when I stood on the roof of our temporary corporate housing looking out at Elliott Bay on a sunny afternoon, I turned to my husband with a huge grin and it immediately felt like home.

Having arrived without a plan of my own, I took a part-time job at a small restaurant while I looked for a more permanent position. I'd been obsessed with food all my life, having grown up in a family of gourmets and having been born in Louisiana, where every life event revolved around the table. Cooking was the one occupation I felt completely competent at without any formal training, but in the food jobs I had worked in Texas, I always felt somewhat marginalized for my lack of a culinary degree. Seattle in the summer, though, with its heavy concentration of tourists, was an easy place for anyone clean and reliable to find kitchen work.

The owner who worked the line alongside her staff of three was a flagrant violator of the most critical health department regulations and had devised a routine to cover up the evidence the second she got the signal that an inspector had arrived. Everyone was to put on gloves, hide the bacon and quiche that usually sat out all day, and move the deli meats away from the raw chicken they shared space with in the cooler. When I anonymously reported her, fearing that she was going to kill someone with the boiled eggs she scraped free of mysterious furry stuff, she convinced the inspector that someone was making up vicious lies and shot me a look that told me my days were numbered. The tip-off was probably that I had always insisted on wearing gloves, which she rationed because of the expense, and because I would point out that the cooler was hovering at fifty degrees, which could possibly explain why the horseradish was hairy. She topped her bottled dressing–tossed Caesar with slices of precooked breaded chicken patties, which customers complained were not what they'd had in mind. And so when her food sales guy suggested a swap of prepared chicken strips with "grill marks imprinted to give the impression of a fresh product," she agreed to the slightly higher price. Her restaurant was some distance from

Pike Place Market, which I would walk by each day, picking up something from the Fish Market or Don and Joe's Meats and vegetables from Frank's for that night's dinner, items better and cheaper than the packaged food my employer was passing off as her own.

So when I saw an ad for a sorority chef at the University of Washington, it didn't occur to me that I was taking a step down by applying. Before I found my way to the Alpha Sigs, I interviewed with the house mother at Delta Delta Delta, a slender fiftysomething blond in white linen trousers and a light sweater buttoned up to her neck. There were far fewer sororities on campus than fraternities, seventeen to thirty-two, but most were much larger, with over a hundred members compared to an average of fifty-five at the fraternities. And they really were two different worlds, the sororities being highly regulated and regimented, the houses formally landscaped, their interiors spotless and decorated in keeping with the well-maintained exterior architecture. The fraternities were more like a collection of guys living at a dive bar furnished by Goodwill, their Greek-columned façades fooling the casual observer.

Having never heard the term "house mother" before, I assumed the job of living full-time with a hundred college girls—while presumably not involved in any sort of intimate adult relationship of your own—was something you did late in life as an alternative to assisted living. But my interviewer explained that this was her vocation and that she had worked at various institutions around the country for most of her professional life. Tri Delts had fired both the former house mother and the cook a few weeks earlier and I gathered that these were not entirely separate incidents, but one more case of a Greek cook and a bored house mom making up for the lack of standard employee benefits by creating a few of their own. The previous cook had left in the summer, believing that he would return in the fall, "and still this is how he left things," she told me as she swept her arm across the basement storage room. She was appalled at the lack of order, but I was appalled at the stacks of gravy mix and powdered hollandaise. "He went many, many thousands of dollars overbudget," she explained as the primary reason for his dismissal, something she obviously regarded as a failure of discipline and I saw as a failure to cook anything requiring more than the addition of water. "I'll work closely with the chef on the menu and budget," she stressed, which I distinctly heard as "I do all the thinking around here."

The kitchen was as big as our first apartment in Seattle, with several ovens, a Hobart mixer, and a separate prep kitchen, and she assured me that there would be plenty of help from houseboys. It was the first time I'd heard the term and it immediately conjured images of servants in colonial India bringing tea to their memsahibs. It turned out I wasn't far off because houseboys were in fact guys from the less well-off fraternities hired to serve the sorority members and wash their dishes. "Do any of you work as houseboys?" I asked one of my Alpha Sig guys later and he told me that one or two had, that some guys would boast about how their new job was going to give them access to tons of hot girls, and how actually it was a mistake. "You see them in their makeup-free, hungover state and they see you as the hired help who sees them in their makeup-free, hungover state. It's just not pretty."

I knew that I had failed the interview when she asked me if I would consider the alternate opening of weekend brunch cook, a job that paid less and required working on the two best days of the week. Given that I was now living child-free in a vacation destination, I was not about to trade my weekend mornings for dawn omelet prep, no matter how interesting I suspected the postmortem conversation in a sorority house must be after Friday and Saturday nights. She later emailed the usual polite rejection with an explanation that she had found someone more qualified, but she did mention that I was still in consideration for the shitty job. I had previously worked as a private chef to a Dallas business owner, a billionaire with a square footage about the size of our subdivision and a household staff sufficient for minor royalty, and I had an unlimited budget to create elaborate meals to please the biggest asshole I've ever met. But I had never heated up canned spaghetti sauce for a hundred college girls, ever. So instead, she hired a male chef who, two years later, walked off the job after finding the ladies of the house had broken into the kitchen and conducted an improvised pillow fight with bags of flour and sugar—not that I felt any malicious satisfaction about this.

"Bring food," a chef friend advised when I told him about the Tri Delt rejection and an upcoming interview with the Alpha Sigs. I had lost confidence by the failure to secure a position that seemed to require no cooking skill whatsoever, but my friend was certain that a fraternity would be different. Guys fending for themselves over the summer would be hungry and vulnerable to the sight of something other than Froot Loops and frozen pizza and would not care a whit about details like experience, qualifications, and references. The job ad had requested a submission of menu ideas, a hopeful sign that these guys put a premium on real food and were looking for someone creative. So I submitted a list of the kinds of simple home-cooked dishes I had served as a private chef:

GARLIC AND SUN-DRIED TOMATO–CRUSTED
CHICKEN WITH ROASTED BROCCOLI

MUSTARD-MARINATED FLANK STEAK WITH
CRÈME FRAÎCHE MASHED POTATOES

HONEY BALSAMIC–GLAZED PORK TENDERLOIN
WITH NUTTED WILD RICE

"Are you available Tuesday or Wednesday at two?" was the immediate response from Bob, the guys' volunteer adult adviser, who lived off-site and had a separate career. And so I arrived for my interview, pot roast and twice-baked potatoes in my arms, waiting at the door that someone had left invitingly wide open for me, and yet feeling suddenly ridiculous and out of place with my homespun wares, like an Amish housewife bringing friendship bread to a biker party.

The Alpha Sig House was on the corner of Forty-Seventh Avenue and Nineteenth Street, which put it two blocks away from the better-known Greek Row on Seventeenth Street that led directly to the main campus entrance. But it wasn't in the Siberia of Twenty-First Street or farther east and it wasn't one of those "houses with letters on it" that was really more like a collection of roommates. The House itself was grand from the exterior, set up on a slight hill with white Greek columns and red brick, three stories high with the fraternity's letters in gold above the front door. Some of the houses on the street were more modern in architecture and some looked more like dentist offices, but from the back on Twentieth Street, all of them were equally nondescript, littered with the guys' vehicles and the numerous Dumpsters required, which completely erased the sense of grandeur of their facades.

I had to ring the doorbell and wait some time at the sorority, but even with the welcoming open door here I felt anxious, and just as I was about to quietly slip away, I saw Bob for the first time, beaming and gesturing, assuring me that it was safe to enter. I relaxed a little when I saw a face with lines at the corners of his eyes and touches of gray around his temples, and as we toured the House he pointed out the composite photograph of his own pledge year, in which he had the same late seventies haircut and wide lapels as the others who were not apparently dropping out and dropping acid. It was impossible to tell who in that group had succeeded or failed or who still knew the secret handshake, but the man standing next to me gazing at the framed photograph had basically never left. He had grown up, though, and was living in nearby upscale Laurelhurst, working long, odd hours as the auditor of Virginia Mason Medical Center and volunteering equally long hours steering the guys through the grown-up details of running a household and now, once again, hiring a cook.

It was Bob who had placed the ad, but unlike at the sorority, hiring authority fell to the members of the House leadership, mainly Alex, the treasurer. Alex was a junior at the time and a student in the respected Foster School of Business. He had fought with the fraternity Corporation Board for an on-site cook after suffering through two years of the worst of institutional meals, which were dropped off daily in foil containers by a cook who prepared meals for several houses. While I sat in the Solarium waiting for the formal interview, Alex was on the phone to the current president. He was clearly annoyed that the supposed head of the House was not around to participate in what Alex obviously saw as the most important choice the guys would make all year. Finally giving up, he called in lesser members of the leadership team, who cared deeply about food, including Meaker, then house manager.

With his rosy-cheeked round face and beard, gentle demeanor, and inattention to fashion, Meaker seemed to me like something of a living teddy bear, a really well-loved and slightly worn-out one. He looked a little older than he was, so at first I thought he was a junior Bob, a kind of house dad, when he was in fact a senior and just one of the guys.

"He had this thing he called Asian Surprise," Meaker told me. "Surprise all right. Bad one. And we told him we hated it. Don't make that again. How much clearer can you be? And he kept sending it to us. We couldn't tell what anything was by looking at it, but we knew from the smell that we didn't want it," he went on. And so many foil containers went straight into the trash unopened that a majority of the guys revolted, refusing to pay a portion of their house bill for food they wouldn't eat.

Despite explicit warnings, the cook was surprised and enraged when they let him go and made one last trip to the House to collect equipment he claimed as his own from previous years when he had cooked in-house, leaving a couple of warped pots and sheet pans and a sign listing his menu for a special dinner: STEAK, BOILED CORN ON THE COB, BOILED BROCCOLI, BAKED POTATO. I was pretty sure from all other indications that the steak had been the cheapest variety he could find, that the corn and broccoli had been frozen, and that the potatoes were accompanied by fake bacon. It was a dismal and uninspired menu but probably a welcome departure from Asian Surprise.

The interview was more like a leisurely after-dinner conversation with good friends and it seemed they were more intent on convincing me of the sanity of choosing this job than in establishing my qualifications. "The guys will treat you with respect," Alex had said, a fact I had not questioned until he planted the idea of anything less in my head. And as I told them that my hope was to bring the same kind of home-cooked meals they were accustomed to, there were a couple of blank looks, but Bob beamed as if envisioning platters of roast chicken and mashed potatoes passing between us. Any anxiety I'd had evaporated as we chatted and various unnamed guys poked their curious heads into the room as if I were already the newest addition to the zoo.

They interviewed me for an hour and a half before nervously showing me what they were calling a kitchen: a three-hundred-square-foot box with one refrigerator that appeared to be (and was) in its last weeks of life, a home freezer with duct tape holding the door in place, a nonfunctioning pizza oven that hogged what little space there was, and an archaic gas range that I later learned would burn the outer three inches of anything placed within. There were a few pieces of barely serviceable cookware, but not so much as a spoon or spatula anywhere. "We know it needs work," Bob had offered in massive understatement. And it was clear from their unconvincing "it's not *so* bad" expressions that they feared this was the deal breaker. But instead of making my escape right then, I asked to see the rest of the House.

The main floor included the kitchen, a large dining hall with six long, wooden tables, a glassed-in room romantically called the Solarium, a study, a TV room, and the entry, centered by a large real fireplace over which hung historical photographs. This was the civilized part of the house, where only alumni and parent parties were permitted and where it was reasonably safe to give tours to doubtful parents of prospective freshmen. The basement, besides being a party location, held the supersecret Chapter Room behind large double doors through which only brothers could pass. And there were two bathrooms, one of which Bob assured me would be mine. On the second floor were the porches and large dormitory-style rooms with bunk beds for the pledges. And on the third floor most of the older guys lived in single or double rooms that they decorated themselves—some of them impressively—with wood flooring and furniture that obviously hadn't come with a FREE sign attached.

I intended to leave my home-prepared meal for them to eat later, but as we wrapped up, Alex asked about the food like a good business major obtaining all the relevant information before making a decision—not to mention just being plain hungry. At that point, several guys who'd not been part of the interview suddenly appeared like starving feral cats. Before I started cooking professionally, I was hesitant to cook for people I didn't know well. When calls went out at church for meals to aid an ailing member, it didn't occur to me that they would just be glad for a goddamn grilled cheese sandwich. Instead I worried about whether they would prefer my coq au vin to my stuffed pork chops and so I would tie myself in knots of obsessive indecision, forgetting that it was not about me. I felt that same anxiety as I looked at the eager faces of these guys and wondered if I'd seasoned the beef well enough and if there was enough butter in the potatoes. But they ate happily in front of me, loving it all. Obviously they were as smitten as I was, and I found them warmer and more insecure than I had imagined.

Phil and I were living in a downtown apartment when I interviewed at the Alpha Sig House. Bob seemed to love the fact that I'd chosen the Cobb, a 1910 Beaux-Arts building, in keeping with his own fondness for history and tradition. He'd been the guys' adviser for twenty years and had lived in the Alpha Sig House when every night was formal, the House was kept clean 24/7, and dinner was always formally plated, facts he would later cite to me nostalgically when all I really hoped for was a clean tasting spoon minus the usual peanut butter encrustment.

Two days after my interview he called to arrange a meeting with Alex and him at a Starbucks near my new home. Along with an employment contract, Alex carried a purple-and-gold bouquet so enormous that other customers turned to stare and we had to place it on the floor while we talked. I kept the matching bow from those flowers and hung it in the dry storage area, where years later, limp and dusty as it was, it reminded me of the oversize love I'd felt at that coffee shop. I would look at it hard whenever I was having the sort of day that required reminders. They had chosen me over a culinary school graduate they had rejected as somehow wrong. It's hard to identify the qualities that make someone *right* for this job, but showing up with a hot meal had obviously trumped arriving in chef whites with nothing but a résumé in hand.

The guys were aware of something that I would only learn later, that some of the "real" professionals at other houses—the ones who wore toques and whites and insisted on being called executive chef—were serving frozen pizza and packaged Alfredo sauce, lamely claiming that's what the customer wanted. It never occurred to me to cede power like that and my answer to requests for garbage was simply, "No, that's garbage." I treated them like they were kids who didn't know better—which they mostly *were*. So I accepted the job knowing that the bar was so low I'd have to work superhard to disappoint.

Years later, when there were no longer any guys in the House with memories of "cat meat and rat meat" dinners, I worried that they had grown jaded, until one of them would send me a text saying, "So I'm at Alpha Alpha and their dinner is: canned chili with melted cheese on top, frozen cornbread and Rice Krispies. SO DIRT." Some of the blame for this lay squarely at the feet of the students themselves, the parents, and the Corporation Boards who wanted to pay low wages and spend minimally on food and then were surprised that they could only attract "drunks and ex-cons, mostly," as one food industry friend put it. But I also wondered about the people who took those jobs without the professional self-respect to demand more of themselves. It seemed to me that if you were hired as a cook, you ought to at a minimum *cook* something.

Three years into the job, a reporter asked me to list some of the more elaborate meals that I prepared, and I explained that a restaurant experience was never my goal; instead just making my own salad dressing in this setting was revolutionary. Boiling macaroni and making cheese sauce, with *cheese,* and sautéing onions and garlic for a marinara instead of opening a can were the kinds of things that seemed like minimal accomplishments to me until I would receive a delivery intended for another house and be dumbstruck by the amount of crap that was passing for food—canned vegetables and whole entrees in a box with dozens of "stabilizing" and "enhancing" ingredients—not a fresh green thing or a raw product to be found.

Early on, I sent an email to the forty other cooks in the Greek community suggesting that we all get together and swap ideas and inspiration, only to learn that there was already a tightly knit group formed whose idea of mutual support was to call each other when the health inspector was in the area—no inspiration sharing necessary when no cooking was required. There were people who'd been doing the job for twenty years, somehow convincing their customers that stirring oil and vinegar together was an unreasonable expectation. And there were others who hopped from house to house every second year after being fired for smoking weed by the Dumpsters instead of for any culinary failings, so it seemed to me that the real reason for bad food was that the people eating it had exceedingly low expectations.

I knew when I took the job that "frat boy" was shorthand for "arrogant, drunk, and disorderly," but I had limited personal experience with an actual fraternity and guessed that the guys who lived in these communities were probably not very different from other college kids and possibly more socially well adjusted. I was pretty sure that the guys who went on campus killing sprees were no one's pledge brother and

suicide seemed to be much more of a concern for dorm RAs than for fraternity presidents. I had seen *Animal House* so long ago that I had only vague memories of guys in sheets and a general negative impression that I knew was probably exaggerated by isolated news stories. And so, just as I rejected the assumption that food served to them had to be one step above Dickensian workhouse gruel, I kept an open mind about my new customers, willing to accept the possibility that they might be individual people who liked food.

But it's not as if the guys who hired me were universally cheering me on in my one-woman revolt against the processed food industry. There were those who asked for "normal" ranch dressing and "regular" lettuce, and who complained of having to Google the items on my posted menu to find out what they were eating for dinner. It was especially galling when they would declare a preference for the frozen sausages at a sorority brunch over the raw pork and apple ones that I had to cook myself, or some other dish that required nothing more of the cook than the ability to turn an oven knob and set a timer. My response was to insist that I was right and to plow ahead, oblivious to the negative.

I had no formal training and no aspirations to climb the culinary ladder, so I didn't share the disdain I would later encounter when I met real chefs who treated me with contempt when they learned where I worked, even if they themselves were dishing out wings and mozzarella sticks at Applebee's. There's a hierarchy in the business and frat cook falls somewhere beneath nursing home and day-care kitchen help, and I could understand this when I started to hear stories about the cooks at other houses in the Greek system. "Most of them are rather fond of the herb," my milk guy told me, and I knew he

wasn't referring to fresh basil. My food sales guys told me stories about male cooks at sororities sleeping with the customers, and female cooks getting liquored with the guys, and the sort of personal drama that explained the clause in my contract stating that "gross misconduct or theft of any kind" was a cause for immediate termination, which I had thought was rather obvious. But apparently there were many who saw stealing and misbehaving as perks that made up for the lack of health care benefits and industry respect.

I'm not sure if it was naïveté or defiance that made me accept the job, but there was something appealing about the challenge and something refreshing about the freedom to make it all up as I went along, casting off long-held notions of what was possible. When times were very trying in the House, when I cut my hand on party-related broken glass or found the freezer inexplicably unplugged for the third time and had to install a *childproofing* device to stop it, I would question whether I even cared if I were right. But then I would think of that wide-open door and those smiles over pot roast and potatoes, and that enormous bouquet wooing me to take this on, and I would remember that nothing I experienced here was ever as bad as the job I'd held just before this one.

Interview Pot Roast

When my grandmother Genevieve Thomas Evans was 101, my younger brother, Eric, videotaped her describing the food she had cooked when we were kids, the kind of simple, real food that I hoped to bring to the Alpha Sig House. This is her description of beef pot roast, which could just as easily be pork or lamb shoulder, and is the basic method I used for all large, inexpensive cuts of meat:

"First you buy a beef roast, a cheaper cut is good, chuck is good, about 3 to 3½ pounds. And then you season it with salt and pepper and brown it real good in some fat in a Dutch oven. You take it out and you put bell pepper and onion and a little garlic in the fat you browned the roast in and then you cook that until it's done, not burned or anything, just done. And then you put your roast back in there and you pour some water, about a cup I guess, and then you cover it and put it on the stove and let it cook on low for hours. Just once in a while, pass through the kitchen and check on it. You get it good and tender. Put more water in there if you need to. Then you lift the roast out and you put potatoes and carrots and seasoning in there and cook them until they're tender and then you put it all back together and it's ready to serve with rice.

"My grandchildren really loved it. We'd make it on a Saturday so you could just heat it up after church on Sunday. And it was easy and good the next day. That's the main thing: Look out for the next day."

2

Domestic

Before taking the job at the Alpha Sig House, I was living two thousand miles away in more ways than one. I'd had kids right out of college, just barely in my twenties, and for the most part, I stayed at home. But when high school graduation was nearing, I was determined to have an identity beyond wife and mom. We were living in the Dallas suburb of Plano, Texas, at the time and the cookie-cutter megahouses and upscale retail environment held little appeal for someone more interested in experiences than stuff. I wanted something more interesting to do with my days than shop and was determined to avoid the depression I'd seen in a lot of stay-at-home moms who suddenly found themselves without a purpose when the kids headed out the door for good.

So I took the first job I could find in the food business, an $8.25 an hour position at the newly opened Central Market, a food lovers' paradise of a grocery store with a high-end prepared foods section and a kitchen employing dozens of cooks and chefs. I talked my way into the catering kitchen, but when management presented us with a book of pictures of just exactly how the vegetables needed to be arranged, complete with weights for every stick of carrot or pile of broccoli, I decided I was a supremely bad fit for the job and started a personal chef business. It was during this period that I responded to a job ad for a private chef to an extremely wealthy family, and it was the voyeuristic fascination that kept me there beyond the point when a rational person like my husband would have been out of there.

The "Robertsons" (a name, like that of all their family, friends, and staff, I've invented) lived in an exclusive section of Dallas, now home to former president George W. Bush, but then also populated by the likes of Ross Perot and the owners of the Mavericks and the Cowboys, the Stars and the Rangers. After passing an initial interview with the HR manager of Mr. Robertson's company, I sat outside my future employer's office an hour and a half past our scheduled meeting time, eavesdropping on whispered conversations about major acquisitions, lawsuits, and, sprinkled here and there, references to the man I was waiting and waiting to see. When I finally did meet him, he seemed to wonder why I was there and I started to wonder, too. Food, I came to realize, was not of much interest, but it needed to be there and that required a cook. He didn't look me in the eye once during our half-hour conversation, but I must have been acceptable because a day later I prepared a test meal for the immediate family and their live-in nannies.

That I can't recall a single dish I prepared for them that night is telling, but it was good enough to have me sitting in the library of their estate afterward for further questioning by

Mr. Robertson and his much younger wife. I assumed that she was employed herself, or the chair of some major foundation, or *something*, because she required an entire staff of cleaners, assistants, managers, maintenance people, gardeners, and a cook. But Mrs. Robertson's job was being massaged, facialed, and lunched, followed by great amounts of sleep to recover. As defensive as it sounds to say that the rich are miserable, I really had never met anyone I envied less. None of the employees spoke ill of her, feeling instead sincerely sad for her: a woman with everything in the world except purpose, exactly the kind of woman I was striving not to be.

During the interview, I declared that while I was willing to work Christmas Day, I wanted to spend Thanksgiving with my family. And while they acquiesced, Mrs. Robertson coughed slightly and shifted uncomfortably in her seat as she looked over at her husband and I realized sometime later that this was the first in a series of transgressions; servants did not dictate schedule. I learned of a summer home out west that would require my services and a private jet that I would need to supply with food. And on this point, I imagined celebratory boxed lunches of lobster cocktail and warm vegetable grain salads, but later learned that the family required an austere tuna salad with minimal mayonnaise along with plenty of Lay's potato chips. In retrospect, I can't imagine why they hired me or why I wanted the job, except that it was interesting to me, despite—or probably because of—the obvious vanity of these employers and the dysfunction of their personal lives. It was never going to be boring, and besides, there was something seductive about a limitless credit card to use completely budget-free.

After my interview, house manager Linda led me through the main living quarters, the extensive grounds, the guesthouse that included a pool, a massage room, and a kitchen even better equipped than the one in the main house, and finally to a building at the edge of the estate, a little one-room shack that the former cook had occupied and that I was welcome to live in with my husband and one son who was still at home. At the time, Phil was an engineer with Hewlett-Packard and we were comfortable if not entirely happy in our suburban castle. The new home on offer was about the size of our garage and appeared to be built of scrap lumber and tin—slave quarters, basically. So I politely declined, the second of my fatal transgressions in a single day.

They told me very little about the previous cook, but there were several mentions of her extreme bouts of depression. "She brought us all down with her," one of the nannies had told me. And having seen the condition of her living space, I'm surprised she didn't do worse than make them all a little sad. Apparently she had gotten along terrifically with the children, who missed her and never quite warmed to me, and had been an adequate cook, but she'd been extremely anxious about large events and well, again, was just not *happy* enough.

Apart from business dinners, teas, and miscellaneous other events, my job was to cook lunch and dinner for the family five days a week and lunch on Saturdays. "We sometimes attend church and do our own thing on Sundays," Mrs. Robertson had declared at the interview in a way that suggested she thought I might be disappointed with less than a seven-day workweek. I was also to cook for a few of the staff, but not the maids, the butler, Charles, the handyman, Roy, or the gardener and his team of laborers. Okay, I was only to offer food to a certain category of staff, like the nannies, Linda, and Mrs. Robertson's personal assistant, Tara. The maids sat together to eat their home-cooked lunches and would sometimes offer me tastes of their Korean vegetable pancakes and their chili pastes and seemed to have no interest in the Kraft singles and fat-free yogurts reserved for family and *certain* people. It was the same with the gardening staff, whose tacos of fresh corn tortillas I could smell when I passed them on my way to the vegetable garden. No Wonder Bread for you!

Despite their work in the Dallas sun, the gardening staff had an enviable freedom from the oppressive household atmosphere, where the nannies acted as surrogate owners, haughtily micromanaging the jobs of lesser employees. I suppose this was inevitable when their main role was to look after the children who were out of the house for most of the day. They clashed constantly with the housekeepers, who were a society unto themselves and followed a strict tradition of obedience to their elders regardless of job title. So when a new maid was hired and happened to be older than the rest, she sat with her feet up, refusing to clean toilets and insisting that the other women serve her tea. I wasn't paying their salaries, so I watched with amusement until the schedule had the elder assisting at parties with no one younger to do the actual assisting. This left me with twice the workload and a sullen woman sitting with her arms crossed, frowning at my refusal to play along. I had trouble reconciling my independent and rebellious nature with these women who complied respectfully with every petty command of their employers and longed to see them rise up in protest. And I was horrified when I learned that they were to wear little French maid outfits at a holiday party, that this was not a joke, but that a rental service was sending them over. I don't know if there is anything more humiliating than requiring sturdy middle-aged women to stuff themselves into black-and-white mini-dresses with their customary black ankle socks and thick-soled shoes, and I wondered what could possibly be the intent, because sexy it was not.

Mr. Robertson had grown up poor in another state and had rejected everything about that experience except a taste for the very simple country foods of his childhood. There were not many endearing things about the man, but the fact that he kept an extensive vegetable garden on the estate and maintained it himself—hard, backbreaking work in the Texas heat—left an anomalous impression. In the house, there was great friction, but when we would happen upon each other in the garden, examining the size of the eggplant or determining if the asparagus was done for the year, all of that vanished and we spoke almost like friends. I had a credit card to spend with abandon at any shop in Dallas, and could order food from anywhere in the world, but I most loved the bounty of that garden and would work Jerusalem artichokes and squash blossoms into menus despite the protestations of their kids, who preferred dinners of grilled skinless, boneless chicken breasts and white rice.

One of the nannies was a vegetarian, uncommon for Dallas and a welcome challenge for me. She told me that she had simply made do by leaving out the meat in previous years, but I tried to accommodate her in more interesting ways with Roasted Red Pepper Tart, Wild Mushroom Crepes, and Wheat Berry Salad with Fresh Mozzarella. She appreciated the effort for a while before finally letting me know that, really, steamed green beans were fine.

As Christmas approached, hordes of presents arrived daily and Tara would make a note of the sender and confer with Mrs. Robertson on whom to regift the mostly unneeded and unwanted items. A cheese-of-the-month gift was awarded to me, the family preferring fat-free shredded cheddar to the Époisses and the bleu d'Auvergnes. Each month I looked forward to the little box, one of the small perks of a job that paid surprisingly little and required extreme holding of my normally rather loose tongue. I was required to work Christmas Day, as were most of the staff, and having grown up watching *Upstairs, Downstairs*, I assumed that there would be similar gracious thankfulness of the masters toward their dutiful servants. I had this ridiculous notion that we would be lined up and handed discreet envelopes of cash before preparing the family feast, but not only were none of us awarded with any sort of token of appreciation or bonus, we were also not wished a Merry Christmas. And of course that's because we weren't *having* one.

In addition to the regular staff, Mrs. Robertson relied heavily on her friend Joanna to decorate and shop and do all of the hostess things that she herself was too busy having pedicures to do. The maids hated her because she carried herself with such an air of superiority and greeted them condescendingly with "Hola!" no matter how many times I reminded her that they weren't Hispanic. I liked her though. Because for all of her aloofness, she was a hard worker and had genuine talent and taste. It was fun to work parties with her because she set gorgeous tables and appreciated food in a way that my employers did not, asking me to make her a snack of stuffed turbot and inquiring with true interest into my menu ideas. She also once invited me to join her for an exclusive cooking lesson at a fine French restaurant, not because she ever lifted a sauté pan, but because she liked the idea of it and knew that I might actually make the caviar-topped custard-filled eggshells. It wasn't that the Robertsons were cruel; they just seemed completely oblivious to the fact that their staff had lives apart from catering to them. But Joanna knew that I was educated and well traveled and had a life that was not so very unlike her own—the difference being that I was happy.

For all of their millions, the family's daily diet was surprisingly mediocre. I kept the fridge and pantry stocked with processed food and low-fat snacks and fat-free cream cheese, and while Mrs. Robertson was rake thin, the nannies carried a great many excess pounds that you didn't see in the staff members who were eating their poverty meals of bibimbap and pinto beans. The pantry was stuffed with "100-calorie snack packs" and instant oatmeal and when rumors circulated that Coke was several months from launching its diet soda with Splenda, Mrs. Robertson insisted that Tara call the company and demand an early supply. She was dumbfounded by the company's failure to comply, not angry so much as stunned at their ignorance of *who she was*.

The fresh garden notwithstanding, Mr. Robertson insisted on out-of-season fruit and when I complied with blueberries in February, I came into the kitchen one morning confronted with half a dozen Post-it notes tacked on the kitchen cupboards. "Horrible, horrible!" on one and "Tasteless," on another, and "Never serve this to me again!" on a container of one of the offenders in the fridge. That no one should be eating blueberries and tomatoes and plums in February, that those items had to be picked unripe and shipped hundreds or thousands of miles and were therefore doomed to tastelessness from the start, was apparently lost on my employer. They should be perfect because he wished it so and I had failed in my selection. I kept the notes for a while with the thought that I might need to show them to a lawyer, because no one would believe such a thing without seeing it. But being someone who rather liked making trouble, I wrote a terse letter to the couple advising them that I would not tolerate humiliating crazy-ass notes in lieu of civilized conversation. And while they said nothing about the letter and continued on as if nothing had happened, that was the beginning of the end for me as far as they were concerned.

I learned from the house manager that in years past the Robertsons had been heavily involved in the Dallas social scene and that there were many grand events before my time, but in recent years there had been a significant decline in their standing, making the job far less glamorous than I'd imagined. In my year there I catered only one grand event, a dinner for a patron of the arts who was turning eighty, and we settled on a menu that included individual beef Wellingtons and a whimsical dessert duo of angel food and devil's food cakes. I enlisted the help of a chef friend I'd met at Central Market and as I was showing him the gilded grounds, he grabbed me by the shoulders, warning me to "watch your step!" At my feet, within inches of being trampled, was an enormous venomous snake.

Not far from that spot was a pond where the family kept swans, their wings clipped to prevent escape from the property.

I was explaining to my friend as we looked out over the water that the mother had recently given birth and had rejected her young, an aberration, since swans are known to fiercely protect their nests. The Robertsons called in an expert to rectify the problematic situation, and all of the staff followed the story with concern until the day one of the nannies told me that the mother had pecked all her babies to death. "So strange," she had concluded. But to me, it was all sort of biblical, the snake and the infanticide just ominous reinforcing images of the atmosphere in that house.

In the spring, after my very first mammogram, I was diagnosed with noninvasive breast cancer and required surgery and radiation that I arranged around my work schedule to minimize the impact on my employer. When Tara brought an obviously expensive bouquet into the kitchen the day before my surgery, I foolishly assumed that it was for me and made an idiot of myself by giving thanks before learning from a confused Tara that the flowers were to be placed in a room frequented by no one. As I lay in the OR the following day, the surgeon and staff were bobbing to the sound of Three Dog Night's "Jeremiah Was a Bullfrog," the single stupidest song ever written, which I had not heard since I was on a school bus in the second grade. And I couldn't help but think as I counted back from one hundred, "So this is how it ends."

When it did not in fact end, I faced six weeks of daily radiation treatment, which I dutifully scheduled early in the morning so that I could meet my work obligations. I would sit in the waiting room looking at all the patients who were worse off than me, and think how hopeful they looked, how much happier than my employers who took spa vacations to recover from the stress of having nothing to be stressed over. I was in the worst stages of treatment, the part where you feel like you're carrying thousand-pound weights, when Mrs. Robertson announced that her stepson and his wife had just had a baby and required meals, which I was to prepare and deliver daily in addition to my usual tasks. I did it because it was my job but without any love, and I'm sure it showed in the food. It was sometime during those weeks that I noticed a printout from a chef placement firm on Tara's desk, which she awkwardly assured me was research for a vacation or emergency fill-in. Suspicious, I pulled up craigslist and discovered that Mr. Robertson's company had placed an ad for a chef and a butler, apparently finding the two current holders of those positions to be inconveniently having lives of their own. I gave notice immediately, to the annoyance of Mrs. Robertson, who told me it was problematic of me to quit just before they were expecting houseguests. And after putting up with her self-important effrontery one too many times, I simply walked away, forgoing the $1,200 due to me in vacation pay, a large sum to me at the time and nothing to them.

Several months later, Hurricane Katrina struck Louisiana, where I had family, and then my mother suffered serious complications during surgery, so the world around me was beginning to feel not just biblical but positively Job-ish. And as I sat out the hours with my husband in the emergency waiting room, I told him I wanted a better 2006—a happier and fuller life. And in one of those strange, synchronistic moments, an email arrived from a former HP colleague of Phil's who'd become a senior manager at Microsoft. "Would you consider moving to Seattle?"

Korean Marinade for Flank Steak

My first exposure to gochujang, Korean chili paste, was at the Robertsons' estate, where the housekeepers kept it on their dining table and used it like ketchup or hot sauce. Asian marinades like this were a favorite with the guys who told me they could smell it all the way down Nineteenth Avenue on their way back from class.

FOR 10 LBS. OF STEAK:

2 cups soy sauce
6 oz. dark brown sugar
10 garlic cloves, chopped
2–4 Thai chilies, chopped
1 T. sesame oil
a 1½-inch piece of ginger, chopped
3 oz. gochujang (Korean chili paste), or about a cup

Combine all ingredients in a blender or food processor and blend until well mixed. Pour over any tough cut of steak (flank, skirt, flap) and marinate overnight. Remove meat from marinade and grill. The marinade keeps in the fridge for weeks.

3

The New Girl

I'm not sure how long I expected this job to last; the only one I'd held more than two years was Mom, which you couldn't very well quit, although there were times you wanted to. Phil had always been supportive whether I worked or not, so there was little incentive to stick to something I didn't wildly love. My older son, Sean, had pledged a fraternity and I'd been the opposite of a "helicopter" mom, choosing to limit my knowledge to "are you okay, are you happy, and do you have enough money?" And my younger son, Simon, a sociology major, viewed fraternities as hate groups, despite contrary evidence from the brother who'd been exceptionally tolerant of *him*. So there was a fair amount of skepticism about how this was going to turn out.

I barely slept the weekend before my Monday start date at the House. I was confident that I could cook, but the few times that I'd done so for fifty people required days of planning, shopping, and preparation and now I had to do it twice a day, every day, five times a week without a break. I was fairly certain it was impossible and that I would fail. I'd never managed a kitchen this size and knew nothing about ordering food and supplies and inventory management and cost control. And there was no one to train me, or even anyone to question, so I wasn't just slightly terrified of the guys; I was slightly terrified of myself. There's always that new-kid-in-class feeling when you start a job, but I started mine with twenty other new kids, the pledge class of 2006. They had months to learn and adapt and prove themselves acceptable, but I'd signed a contract for a year and wasn't sure I would make it through the first week.

My arrival at the Alpha Sig House was somewhat accidental, but the guys who were there with me had deliberately searched for a fraternity that would serve as a surrogate home. And still, I could not identify a unifying principle around which they had concluded that this was the place they wanted to spend the next four years. They had alternatives like the Christian House and the Jewish House, and the House where you had to pass an income threshold to join. There was one that gave all incoming freshmen a magic sword upon signing. But the fraternity I had joined was hard to label. There were Republicans, Democrats, and Libertarians. There were guys on scholarship, or the debt-for-life plan, and others who wanted for nothing. There were Catholics and Jews, Muslims and atheists. There was an outspoken homophobe and a guy who later came out, to no one's surprise. The only thing that seemed to unify them was that they wore the same letters, and I loved that I had chanced upon the House that I couldn't describe in one word—or ten.

Badley was in that freshman class. He was a relentless optimist, greeting all of my justifiably sarcastic observations with "Don't be a hater!" And he appeared to be more like eight than eighteen with his perpetual rosy-cheeked smile, which was seemingly unaffected by the life thrashings that beat most people down by the time they finish high school. It seemed especially dissonant because there were little signs that he hadn't had a clear path to this place. He had a different last name when I first met him, one that he legally changed abruptly and without explanation shortly after he joined the House, and I always felt that it was one of those things I was never to ask even Bob about, or that if I asked I would get the sort of answer I got about other mysterious goings-on in the House, a confusing, wordy, and polite kind of "no comment." So I assumed facts not in evidence and stayed clear of any questions about Father's Day or family vacations or anything at all about the first eighteen years of his life. And so he always seemed to me just slightly more of a kid than any of the others, and just slightly more my responsibility.

His pledge brother Newman was another who stood out from that freshman crowd, but in a different way, by being much more self-assured than most pledges and so accurately biting in his wit that even the older targets of his barbs couldn't help laughing and loving him. He came from the sort of solid, prominent family and loving parents that made him not just materially taken care of, but radiantly confident and socially gifted. And he was physically attractive on top of it all, which seemed like an unfair stacking of the deck. I assumed that he'd attended the same sort of privileged high school I had, but it meant nothing to me when Bob would tell me that one of the incoming freshmen was a graduate of O'Dea or Bishop Blanchet. Though I guessed by the way he relayed this information that these were not the kinds of schools with metal detectors; I hadn't grown up in Seattle and by the time we moved here I was no longer focused on schools the way we'd been when our sons' needs determined where we chose to live. And it was no more impressive to me that his parents had high-prestige careers. Instead I was taken right from the start by a hundred other things that he did himself, like painting a mural on the basement wall, and leaving encouraging notes overnight on my kitchen door, and lending a hand without pay or pleading, just because he could see that I needed the help.

I'd toured the kitchen with the leadership team at my interview, taking note of the fossilized penne pasta on the worktable and the bowl of uncovered salad in the fridge, slimy and deflated with a spoon left in it in case anyone might be desperate for a bite to eat. So I knew there was work to do before I could think of cooking, and two weeks before my start date, I scrubbed the kitchen and storage areas, the worst being a basement room that evidence suggested had been a dumping ground and a private location for sex that you'd have to have been wasted to enjoy. Leaks from the nearby washing machines spilled in, creating a stagnant pool, and unclaimed laundry sat in heaps next to a sign taped to the wall declaring, CLEAN UP YOUR SHIT. IT'S NOT THAT HARD.

Besides the shelves of long-expired gravy mix and canned green beans, vestiges of a time when someone "cooked" inhouse, there were numerous boxes of garbage that someone had inexplicably placed in storage. And when I pulled out one of those boxes, I found piles of porn magazines, the pages streaked with something black and sticky. As I lifted the pages of perfect female nakedness, I found a stiff dead rat about seven inches long gazing straight up at me, its mouth gaping open. Days later, in another pantry, I faced off with a live one, and then babies in another spot. And just when we thought we had deinfested the place, the health inspector happened to be present when another belly-up specimen appeared in a dark corner of the kitchen. The inspector handed me his report with the annotation, "Nice rat."

Happily though, it was not all chaos and critters, and I discovered that there was a leadership structure in the House, a tradition of order that had gone on for nearly a hundred years on this campus. "Is anyone in charge here?" a new linen service provider had asked me after refusing to haul away a dirty floor mat. I wanted to point out that we were, after all, paying him to *clean*, but instead I said defensively that "*they* are.*" It was different at sororities where house moms and housekeepers and gardeners and dishwashers removed any personal responsibility for order and cleanliness from the inhabitants. Here, it was a mess. But it was their mess. And they would return it to an acceptable condition periodically, either when a tipping point number of them had had enough of eating cereal surrounded by food scraps from three days ago or when I texted the house manager to say, "No clean dining room, no lunch."

Meaker was the house manager the year I started, the same reassuringly teddy bear–like character who had been a part of my interview and had lessened my anxiety with his vivid descriptions of prison-worthy meals from the previous cook. I was standing in the dining room during my first week, feeling— and I suppose looking—overwhelmed and from across the room, he said quietly, "I'm here to help you. Whatever you need." But I didn't know his particular leadership role then and learned it not because of his superior handyman skills (of which he was clearly bereft), but because I would constantly hear "Meeeaaaker!" ringing through the House when someone needed a lightbulb change.

I never actually saw him do anything related to the upkeep of the building, but he was wonderful to me and that defined a good house manager. Ditto for president, vice president (technically my boss), and secretary. The one role that required any competency, as far as I was concerned, was that of treasurer, because he paid the food bills, was trusted with ensuring that my bonus came to me three times a year, and was not allowed to be "creative" with accounting—three tasks that proved challenging for at least one of the treasurers during my tenure.

There were other leadership roles that didn't directly affect me. There were positions like marshal, responsible for pledge education, a term that immediately made me picture all of the freshmen sitting in a windowless room for a brainwashing session, and social chair, a position that often went to the biggest party animal and was wildly popular with everyone in the House except me. And then there were people whom I could count on as "someone who has his shit together more than most." These were people who didn't want to bother with actually running for office, but who couldn't suppress natural leadership qualities. Tony was one of these, a senior capable of balancing a hard-partying schedule with a high level of personal responsibility; he was one of those who didn't think it was okay to excuse every stupid act of destruction with "I was drunk," but instead was often the first person who greeted me in the morning, already aware of what might have me counting to ten. He had unusually high cleanliness standards and believed in logical consequences, sending me home one Friday when he saw the previous night's dishes strewn around the dining hall and the contents of someone's stomach in one of my chafing dishes, with the simple declaration that "we don't get any food today."

The role of recruiting new pledges went to the rush chairs, who received a discount on their housing bill based on meeting goals that were completely unrealistic and who would work hard to reach three-quarters of their target, which was really all anyone expected in the first place. The year that I joined they actually did meet the goal, but only by padding the roster with recruits who would not make it through initiation, either by their own choice or by force. Some were put off by the lack of privacy and some were incomprehensibly surprised to find alcohol readily available or that virginity was not a given. But for the most part it was the work that did them in; it was the discovery that a house this large didn't run itself and required something of them, and that, as I came to understand myself, while I had many titles beyond cook, maid was not one of them. That was *their* job.

My hire date was in late August so I learned about the rush process after the fact. Freshman Badley had wanted to avoid the time-wasting tours of fraternities he was never going to join anyway and implored the president, Charlie, to steer him toward only the very best Houses. And Charlie, displaying Machiavellian leadership skills, handed Badley a list of all the very worst houses, the five or six that had plateaued at thirty members, or couldn't pay their bills, or who were in imminent danger of being dissolved by their national organization. So when Badley paid visits to houses that were falling apart, occupied by guys whose idea of entertaining a rushee was to offer him microwave popcorn and let him watch their video game skills, he was left with a single choice. But most of the guys took their time at ostensibly better houses before ending up where Badley had defaulted, coming to the conclusion that these weren't necessarily the richest or smartest or most attractive, but they were the coolest.

A couple of days after they moved in and several weeks before fall classes began, the guys gathered for Work Week. Early each morning, all of the pledges assembled in the dining hall under the direction of the marshal and divided into groups to return the House to a condition it had not been in since the end of last year's Work Week. But I didn't know this and thought that all of the fixing and scrubbing and painting and trash removal were just meant to tend to a summer of neglect. I thought that the whole year would be like this, that the place would be maintained in military order and cleanliness, just like I believed that the WOMEN'S BATHROOM sign on the door in the basement meant I could have a pee without being barged in on by my customers, who always seemed completely surprised to find me standing at the mirror touching up my lip gloss. "*Women's* bathroom!" I would cry out as I exited every time, as if I thought that *this time* it would make a difference.

Some of the pledges seemed to share my belief that they'd be on their knees scraping spaghetti off the floorboards for the remainder of their serfdom, and moved out before I'd had a chance to learn their names. A few found even the periodic washing of dishes and mopping of the sticky basement to be too much and lasted less than a month. The more committed ones (or those who knew it was too late to get a dorm room) just whined their way through it, doing a half-assed job, with the perverse consolation that the misery would pass on to the next group of pledges. And the guys who did the least and complained the most were invariably the ones who would scream loudest about the poor performance of the pledges once they were no longer one of them.

The very first meal I made for them was a lunch of taco salad, adapting a recipe from *Cook's Illustrated* for taco meat that started with fresh onions and garlic. I laid everything out on the lunch table—all the contrasting colors of fresh produce and sour cream and cheese arranged appetizingly—only to have the hungry mob turn the table itself into a salad plate. My introduction to the pointlessness of presentation was summarized by one of the freshmen, who said, "We're guys. We don't care."

I had chosen taco salad because it seemed like the most uncontroversial dish possible. But I hadn't considered that for many of these guys, just as it wasn't macaroni and cheese if it wasn't neon orange, it wasn't a taco if you could identify particular food particles in the meat mixture. Badley let me know right away that there were never going to be safe choices here, not in a house this size. "Well, I'm really not too sure about all those onions," he said warily standing in my kitchen to witness twelve cups of them sliding into a pan the size of my entire stovetop at home. I assured him that raw onions became a very different thing when cooked, but he shook his head as he walked away muttering, "I don't know about that. Have to see for myself." And I wondered what kind of food he'd grown up eating that spared him this ingredient, since almost everything on my menu that week started out the same way.

His pledge brother Newman, though, did not hesitate to pile his plate high with the meat mixture, going heavy on the lettuce and easy on the chips, and was, I would learn, the sort of person who would ask me which *type* of onion I was using, and would peer into the fridge looking for horseradish for his roast beef, and requested truffle oil to drizzle over his pizza. Badley joined him in line, sniffing at his food warily before eventually cleaning his plate, and the rest of their pledge brothers lined up more or less indifferently, as if this were nothing out of the ordinary. But in another part of the dining hall were the ones who'd hired me, Alex and Josh and Meaker, and they knew better, Alex remarking about the beef that tasted like meat and the lime juice that came from a fruit.

It was those older guys who explained the culture, not just to the pledges but to me, there being daily discoveries of strange new things, like the complete absence of a female presence on the streets in the first days of the school year. The sororities kept the girls locked up and so the guys had the double punishment of having to labor all day cleaning the House without hope of female company at the end of it. I couldn't help thinking of hundreds of Rapunzels confined to their Greek columned mansions when I heard the term "locked up," and senior Josh reinforced that notion when he let me know with great excitement that "they're letting the girls out today!" Josh was the vice president at the time, one of several African Americans in the House and one of those who'd gleefully sat in on my interview. He'd given me numerous menu suggestions, reassuring me that I couldn't possibly do worse than my predecessor. I learned early on that he was not just a lover of food but of the ladies as well when I found a letter discarded in my pantry signed by three of them explaining what they'd like to do with him that left little ambiguity. So his excitement at their release was understandable and while they waited, the brothers taught the pledges amazingly vulgar songs that they would practice in the entry hall, many of them turning bright red when I walked by and heard snappy new versions of "Row, Row, Row Your Boat" and "Mary Had a Little Lamb."

I had started my own Work Week, which turned into Work Months, before the freshmen had even moved in. And once the hard labor was over, the cleaning out of the cobwebs and rat-infested porn, I took a hard look at the systems in place that I thought were probably sucking money out the door needlessly. Because no one had really been in charge of the kitchen, there was no oversight of vendors and the guys just paid bills for services they weren't even sure they were getting. No one had told me to do this and I realized suddenly that as little as I knew about running a professional kitchen, the guys knew very much less. And it was clear in my first few months on the job that those vendors were both nervous about a change in kitchen management and counting on my inexperienced little lady appearance to keep the status quo.

First to go was a "local" meat supplier, local only in the sense that the company had an office a few miles from campus. "But where are you sourcing your meat?" I asked. He didn't seem to understand the contradiction when he told me rather proudly that it was from Kansas, eighteen hundred miles away. "We're a Seattle-based business!" he stressed again and it annoyed me that he was either stupid or thought I was. When I finally grew tired of the conversation, I told him that I would not be needing anything from him, now, next week, or possibly ever. "But we've been doing business with this House for years!" he complained. And I learned that there were certain vendors all of the houses in the system worked with and because no one had ever questioned this, an air of entitlement hung over them. But I was the new girl and didn't know or care about the rules, and Bob had told me I could choose my own team.

When the dishwasher began to shake so violently that it appeared to be making its own exit from the House, I learned that we could both save money on chemicals and obtain a new one by ditching the company the guys had leased from for as long as anyone could remember. I then informed Joe that we would not be needing his services or his aging, leaking machine any longer. Joe, who weighed a hundred pounds more than I did and had at least eight inches on me, took it rather badly. Standing less than six inches from my face, he told me I was making a very big mistake, thinking I suppose that it was a good last-ditch sales tactic. For a moment I actually did feel physically threatened, but it was also the first of many times that I stepped back and realized, "I work in a house packed full of young, strong, fearless guys who are on my side." And it was like suddenly discovering you have superpowers.

I was ready to fire our main food and supply purveyor, too, over a series of errors, and had already set up an account with the competition when Rod appeared unannounced to apologize and to plead his case. I'd met him a couple of times and I knew him superficially. He was about my age, an aspiring corporate food executive who lived away from Seattle in the more conservative Eastside, and he drove a brand-new big-ass truck. These were the kinds of demographic details that I was quick to put negative labels on. As a district sales manager, he was too senior to spend more than a couple of polite minutes with the cook of a minor account, so when he stood in the doorway humbly asking for a minute of my time, I knew that he'd read my tersely worded good-bye to his sales

guy Kirk and concluded that this was a level of pissed off requiring some senior-level attention.

"Did you assign your B team to us because we're a frat?" I
asked, forcing him to stand in the hot kitchen in full suit and
tie while I continued to work. He smiled and assured me that
he had no A team, but he was working on it and we'd be first
in line. I was half listening as he began what I was sure would
be the usual rehearsed sales pitch that I expected would sound
an awful lot like the insincere promises to angry girlfriends I
heard on a daily basis in that House.

Instead he asked if we could sit down for a minute, and
when we did he told me that I was completely right about the
service lapses—no excuses. Asses would be kicked and things
would change. "It's too late," I told him and he leaned forward,
elbows on his knees, pausing before he moved on to what
appeared to be a spontaneous plan B. "Well, I'd like to at least
hold on to your juice business," he said, a completely irrelevant and ridiculous suggestion plucked from out of nowhere,
which could just as well have been "your canned-tomato
business," or "your garbage-bag business," before adding the
even more desperate and unlikely, "I will personally deliver it
to you." I sent him away believing he'd lost the account, only
to call him later the same day to say that I'd changed my
mind. He'd not only avoided the "don't you worry your pretty
little head with that" attitude of the meat and dishwasher
guys; he'd made me laugh by cleverly admitting fault while at
the same time making fun of my badass tough-chick act. I
knew it would be useful both to have the ear of someone
headed for the top and, along with Bob, to have another
grown-up to talk to. Being around twenty-year-old guys all
day long was surely going to wear thin.

I had swiftly exercised the clause in my contract giving me "final say on all purveyors used for the supply of food and related services," but there were a number of rights of the chef that I learned were not absolute guarantees so much as impractical promises. They included things like: "Chef has the right to cancel meals in the event of repeated violations of necessary sanitary standards and/or problems caused by unauthorized kitchen usage by undergraduates."

Had I strictly enforced this particular right, I'd never have cooked a single meal, and I learned after several attempts at selective enforcement that doing so only made me the bad guy. So I learned to simply not care about any area other than my 120-square-foot cooking environment and insisted on having a lockable door installed between my domain and the dish room and dining hall. It was the first of many strategies I learned that allowed me to remain sane in an environment where leaving food out for days and flushing reams of paper towels ("because we were out of toilet paper") were not considered aberrant behavior.

There were quaint phrases in my contract like the one stating that my parking space "shall be vacant and available on a 24-hour basis." And for the most part, while I came to view this document as aspirational, occasionally I would pull out a copy and furiously underline whole sections about how "chef is not responsible for cleaning of the dining room and snack areas." I would tape my underlined document up for all to see, but I came to understand that the offending parties didn't consider this their responsibility either, so the point was rather lost on them.

For at least half of that first year, I was polite and earnest and customer focused—and all of the things that you are supposed to be in a normal job. When I look back at early emails between Bob and me, I'm not sure who that person was, because I would write out-of-character things like "I don't want to be presumptuous" and "I'm humbled." But really I think I was just insecure, fearful in the beginning much the same way the pledges were, not of the same things—the imagined force-feeding of puke sandwiches and drinking goat blood and other such wild fantasies—but of rejection. It was only later that I realized you have to do something really fucking horrible to be fired from this job and being presumptuous and not exactly humble didn't come close. In time I learned that there were only two qualities that really mattered to these employers: showing up every day and producing great-tasting food. I didn't have to dress or behave a certain way and it didn't matter if I unleashed my tongue, spewing a stream of profanity at them; in fact, this entertained them so long as Rosemary Grilled Chicken with Penne in a Tomato Cream Sauce accompanied the show.

I learned quickly that cooking for fifty guys, a number that would grow to eighty by my fifth year, was not the same as multiplying five by ten. You could make calzones with home-made pizza dough for five and it would be a little project. But if you thought it would just take ten times longer at your new job, you were so very wrong. I learned this when I found myself covering every surface area in the kitchen, including the top of the dishwasher and fridges, with sheet pans of expanding dough, leaving myself with no place to make the filling. And you couldn't just take a recipe for eight and expect it to work for six times that, as I discovered when I put three gallons of cream in a scalloped sweet potato dish and found molten liquid seeping out through the bottom of the ovens onto the floor, filling the kitchen with smoke and the smell of burn-ing marshmallows. I created menus that were so elaborate they required teams of volunteers to execute them. So when soph-omore Eliab remarked that "this cooking is work!" when I had simply asked him to peel fifty pounds of tiny red pota-toes, I knew I had to do a major rethink. Eliab had a positive and energetic personality five times bigger than his small stat-ure and was one of the first to jump into unpaid kitchen labor, so I pouted when he'd said it, aware that he wasn't a whiner by nature and that I was alienating my biggest fans. I was not willing to compromise on scratch cooking, but I couldn't have us all slitting our wrists in the process. Somehow, I thought, there had to be a middle ground between calzone meltdowns and completely copping out.

I learned from the health inspector that copping out was exactly what most were doing when he greeted me on his first visit that fall with, "This won't take long, not too worried about you frat cooks." I was spice-rubbing raw chickens while he spoke about the safety of precooked meatballs and pro-cessed entrees. "You're not actually cooking anything, so no worries," he went on cheerfully, ignoring the contradictory evi-dence before him. I could mock my food salespeople when they tried to sell me the powdered Whisk & Serve Alfredo Sauce, but when a government official barged into your work-place unannounced and uninvited and made proclamations about your craft, you just had to take it. Still, I knew he wasn't talking about me personally and there was probably a reason for his prejudices against cooks in the Greek system; *we were not actually cooking anything.*

If the period between pledgedom and brotherhood seemed long to the freshmen, it was a trial for me, in the medieval sense of the word: subjection to suffering or grievous experience. Having come from a job where the mental challenges were much greater than the physical ones, I knew that cooking five hundred plates of food a week was going to be an adjustment. But having no time off between August and Thanksgiving, with multiple VIP dinners and late deliveries, on top of the sheer slog of standing on my feet all day cooking in such quantity was more like a flogging than an adjustment. So I was not sympathetic to pledges who would ask me if I'd signed a nondisclosure agreement in the hopes I would speak out about the torture they were suffering picking trash off the couches—the same couches on which they were about to plant themselves for a little R&R from the grind of going to classes like Sociology of Sex. "Tell me about it!" I would scream to their bemusement, it having never occurred to them that my salary didn't justify the hours I was putting in to assure them a frozen dinner–free diet, that I was doing this for love of their sorry lazy asses!

Recognizing the strain, Bob suggested that a few of the freshmen rotate as kitchen helpers for a small discount on their house bill and it sounded wonderful to me in principle: twelve hours of assistance from employees with no commute, and therefore no excuses. And because they were in that pledge probation period, there was an added incentive to perform, although, my fearsome reputation notwithstanding, I never did have the slightest say on who made it through initiation. I had a say *after* the fact when I pointed out that I knew all along Jerry was the most slothful person *ever* and they could have saved themselves a lot of misery by asking me before putting themselves through the legal maneuver of removing a brother from the premises. And while I was happy for the indentured servitude, I soon learned its drawbacks. The guys needed more instruction than I had time to give, constantly had class conflicts with their work schedule, and would sometimes claim sickness, only to show up first in line at the dinner buffet, suffering, I was told, from the kind of sickness with which they could still eat and party, just not *work*.

Admittedly I wasn't the easiest boss in those early days before I learned to let some things go and focus on what mattered, before I understood that the guys didn't care if there were a few chopped parsley stems as well as leaves in the jambalaya or if I hand-diced the onions for chili instead of running them through the food processor. Those things might matter in finer places where presentation counted as much as taste, but here they were just hungry and there were a lot of them and only one of me. But in those early days, I insisted on pointless perfection and even a professional chef I knew laughed at me for "torturing those boys" when I told him that I had made my latest helper, Brian, weigh two-ounce portions of the meatball mixture to ensure uniformity, and then mocked him for having some look more like parabolas than spheres. "You're horrible," my chef friend had declared.

Even so, I didn't much sympathize with guys making ten bucks an hour working hours of their choosing in their own home; it wasn't all that hard, not a tenth as hard as *my* job. So while Bob preferred to keep the number of "outsiders" to a minimum and suggested a new set of freshmen workers more to my liking, I insisted on hiring help that didn't live in. Placing an ad online, I learned for the first time what an abundance of lost and desperate humanity there is in the land of "food/beverage/hospitality." Among those who'd gone to a third-rate culinary school with expectations of becoming the next Bobby Flay and those who wanted to "just give those boys a big hug," there was a request from a social worker that I hire a client of hers, a man in his thirties with an undiagnosed personality disorder. And I hired him, because that was my strongest option.

In my defense, I had wanted to do some real good by hiring someone on the margins of society for a job I thought anyone breathing should be able to do, but it was a spectacularly poor decision, given my lack of patience and the immaturity of some of the customers I was asking him to serve. Jim had no filter and would blurt out wild social and sexual questions to guys who were only too happy to overshare. I wouldn't know how to respond to questions like, "Well aren't you a little worried about eating all those beans before your party tonight?" Some of the guys thought it was a great new game, although senior Josh dreaded Jim's questions and when asked things like whether it was necessary to wash your underwear after each wearing would respond that "Tony knows all about that," passing him off to whoever happened to be standing nearby. It didn't matter what the question was; someone *else* was invariably an expert on the subject and it just happened to be the person nearest.

I knew I would have to work around Jim's physical and emotional limitations, but over time he let me know that *everything* was a physical and emotional limitation. It began with knives, which he was afraid of, a fact he demonstrated by shaking uncontrollably and cutting himself on his first day. And then it was sensitivity to temperatures, at first cold, which I learned when he moaned about putting his gloved hands into a bowl of potatoes and mayonnaise to mix that day's salad. Hot came next when he complained that washing dishes was burning his skin. Finally he expressed concern about lifting anything over thirty pounds. So I made a list of the accommodations I needed to make for my new kitchen assistant:

No fruit, vegetable, or meat prep requiring a knife.
No direct contact with anything below fifty degrees or
  above seventy-two degrees.
No standing within two feet of anything on the stove or
  on the grill.
No placing items in or removing them from the oven.
No dishwashing.
No help with the delivery, hauling boxes upstairs.

After several weeks of an ever-shrinking job description, we settled on unloading the dishwasher as safe territory. But multitasking was another challenge I discovered when he insisted on carrying one item at a time from the dish room into the kitchen. When I finally cried, "How many goddamn times do I have to tell you that?" and saw that Jim was pausing to grasp for a number, I knew for certain that it was not working out.

As much as a mercy to him as for my own sake, I let Jim go. I found it hard to know what to say when another employer called for a reference, until I learned that the job in question was not kitchen work and that I could honestly say he had given me perfect attendance. There was no need to elaborate that he had not missed a day of doing nothing I required. My frustrated outbursts had been entertaining to the guys and embarrassing to me, someone who was supposed to be the grown-up in the House, and I felt acute shame that I'd subjected him to an ambiguous world that he took at face value. So I spent the rest of the year working alone, finding it easier to be a martyr than a manager.

I fired Jim just before the Christmas party, so I was on my own for my first major event, the House being small enough that year to hold a silent auction and dinner on-site. These family gatherings were primarily for the parents of the pledges, and were intended to assure them that their sons were still alive and attending class. As he did at the summer barbecue before the school year, Bob made a speech emotionally defending fraternity life, pointing out that these guys were forming bonds that would last a lifetime. He always ended with the kicker that if their grades dropped below a certain threshold, they'd be out the door. This wasn't Animal House; there were standards here.

It was the pledges who provided the items up for bid and it was obvious from the selection which guys had given their parents more than a day's notice. The handcrafted and cellophane-wrapped gift basket containing martini glasses, bar tools, and a cocktail book sat between the Mariners tickets and the Fran's Chocolates, but it all sold, parents buying from each other to pay for major House improvements. I was impressed that without a cattle prod the guys had transformed the basement from its usual frat party status at 3:00 P.M. to a gala event location suitable for grown-ups and siblings by 5:00. Even the "women's bathroom" was what you might be forgiven for thinking it was.

Final exams followed the week after the Christmas party. And it was the last finals week that I made the mistake of cooking for everyone through Friday. No matter how organized the House leadership and I tried to be, it was always the case that the people assigned to clean up were not the same people around to eat the food—the dishwashers were invariably the people with a last final on Monday—and so both dishes and food piled up into a mountain of filth and waste that Bob and I spent several hours cleaning before I went home for two weeks of restoration.

And restoration was essential because the weeklong rites of initiation followed shortly after the New Year. The weeks that led to this were a careful dance of badgering without bullying and instilling terror without actually being terrible. You couldn't force the guys to clean, for example, because that teetered on the edge of hazing. And because true hazing had become the sort of thing that could not only get your House shut down but could also get you arrested, the guys found more innocuous ways to break the spirit and soul of the pledges. The freshmen were required to do anything legal requested of them by a brother. This is how I learned which of the older guys were in my favored column; you could tell a lot by how people in power chose to exercise it. Those who had no interest in even pretend hazing but instead just wanted to get to know the pledges would send them on a scavenger hunt or assign creative tasks like "draw a picture of what you imagine the Chapter Room to look like," that room being forbidden to all but initiated brothers. The brothers who assigned such homework were at the top of my list. And then there were always one or two whose imagination yielded "make me a sandwich" or "take out my trash," which confirmed that my negative snap judgments about them were spot-on.

I imagine Initiation Week was weird enough for the pledges, but for someone on the outside it all seemed scarier and crazier than it probably actually was, like the way psychological thrillers are much more horrifying than straight-up blood and guts. For me, the week went something like this: requests for "the gross parts" of chickens I was butchering, a query into whether I could order a live goat from US Foods, pledges refusing to talk to me for an entire day, strange clothing hung in the basement, locked doors forbidding me access to food-storage areas, and paraphernalia that did not appear to be the stuff of your normal frat party. And then it was over and the pledges who'd made it through, which was almost always everyone—even the ones who'd turn out to be problematic and about whom I'd later say, "I told you so"—became part of the club.

Once they were past that hurdle and obtained the title of brother, the newly initiated split into two distinct camps, thankfully not of remotely equal size: those who really were of great, sound character (the vast majority) and those who were so totally faking it. I could feel this the very morning after the big ceremony, when the latter camp were suddenly no longer doing their jobs or offering to take out that bag of trash instead of going to look for a ladder to climb over it. The former were there in my kitchen like always, unchanged from the day before. And so a different sort of dynamic took over, one in which I could no longer count on a spotless kitchen and many willing hands, but in which I could trust the ones who hung out with me, knowing they didn't have to.

Just after spring break, a new group of pledges moved in, a much smaller group of five. Because they had missed the ceremonies of the fall season—especially Work Week and the ritualistic courting of the sorority girls—and because their period of suffering was very much shorter, subsequent spring pledges seemed to me less committed and more opportunistic. It was as if they had decided to skip all that tradition stuff and go speeding ahead to the bro part. But the five that year stood out from those of later years as something other than casual boarders, and two especially so.

Zach was in this group and immediately bonded with Newman, although in appearance they were opposites. He had wavy brown hair that seemed to have never seen a brush and sideburns and brown-rimmed glasses that made him look like a 1970s college professor. He was, however, just like Newman and Badley in his frequent requests for food treats. He once texted me a request for forty cookies the night before a Thursday class presentation that would be graded by the students and he wanted to "butter them up" with some treats. He texted a second time to make sure I got the joke. He was like that: sure of his wit, but not sure of my appreciation, once bursting into my kitchen to announce that I just had to drop everything and come take a picture of Newman, Dan, and him changing a tire, sweaty and shirtless, as if this were obviously the most interesting thing I was going to see all week. He was just slightly nerdy in that self-conscious way that made him attractive to young women put off by guys who seemed to love themselves most of all. It was because of this that I called him a Man of Mystery, a chick magnet without seeming to try.

Kevin was also in that select spring class. At twenty, he was two years older than your average pledge, emotionally more mature, and not nearly as inclined to do the stupid freshman things that made you want to lock him in the storeroom. Physically strong, he was an enthusiastic player on the House soccer team and a huge music fan. And when he learned that my husband had come to Seattle to work on Zune, Microsoft's challenge to the iPod, he would come into the kitchen to play with the prototypes I brought to work the year before its release. I had expected he might balk at orders from younger guys, but Kevin didn't need orders or lessons in common sense: He was one of those who would see that rice was still sticking to a pan and *not* stack it up with the clean ones, and who, when sweeping the dining hall, would not simply shove the garbage from side to side, clearing a path edged with shredded cheese and broken taco shells. And instead of whining about dish duty, he and his chore partner Julien would crank up the stereo and just get on with it, arguing like an old married couple over who was carrying the most weight, a conversation that went exactly the same way every day and still managed to make me laugh.

Newman had been that kind of pledge and quickly established himself as a leader and House darling, being chosen that spring to represent Alpha Sigs in a competition to be what amounted to "Hottest Greek Guy" for Delta Gamma's sorority fund-raiser for the blind. What this meant in practical terms, he told me, was that he'd have to swear off bread and pasta and gorge on huge quantities of nothing but plain poached chicken and beef and protein shakes, a diet that was supposed to beef up an already buff body and earn him the title of Anchorman. I got the social purpose of this, appreciating the money raised for an absolutely worthy cause, but I found the diet stupid and was vocal about my belief that one day they should have a philanthropy event to correct the health effects of philanthropy events. It made absolutely no difference that the regime never produced an Alpha Sig winner because someone at a competing fraternity would earn the title, presumably because he had a cook more sympathetic and accommodating to scrapping those sabotaging balanced meals.

Along with showing off their hard bodies for judgment by the ladies of Delta Gamma, the contestants were required to perform a synchronized swim, preceded by a skit, with a team of their fraternity brothers. And because we had no pool of our own for practice—unlike some of the more advantaged fraternities—Newman and four of his pledge brothers resorted to using a table as a placeholder for an actual pool as they went over their choreography in the costumes Newman had selected. Being new on the scene, I was unaware of any of this until the afternoon I stumbled upon five of my guys apparently drunk off their asses and dressed in nothing but tight black briefs and firemen hats dancing to "YMCA" around a table. I just assumed I had walked in on one of those secret rituals I was to immediately put out of my mind.

Anchor Splash was just one of the philanthropy events that preceded a cluster of them during Greek Week, a festive time late in the school year that was equal parts a show of unity and proof that fraternities and sororities were not just about keggers and burning couches on Seventeenth Avenue. Really. They were first and foremost about character and community. I fully supported the skits and the car smashes and all of the events that didn't involve eating disorders, but Greek Week I discovered was to become one of my least favorite times of the year, the antithesis to Work Week, and thankfully within a month of summer break.

It began with Morning Bar on Monday, with my usual peaceful 7:00 A.M. arrival assaulted by a thumping beat in the basement and several girls flirting with my completely sober, but totally submissive food delivery driver as he took five times longer than normal to unload. "What the hell?" I screamed at him over the din of an early morning party, as he explained that he was trying but that the path from his truck to my kitchen involved navigating a gauntlet of aggressive, unwanted female attention. My work hours generally spared me a complete picture of the guys' lives, leaving me with a somewhat sanitized view of all but the true alcoholics, except for what I would hear in the kitchen debrief the next morning. But during this bacchanal, I frequently had to lock my kitchen doors to get through the day, because, as anyone who's been sober at a party knows, it's just not that fun for *you*. The rest of the week was pretty much the same, although by Friday most realized the novelty had worn off sometime around Wednesday at noon and the older guys said it wasn't nearly as good as last year, but you got the feeling that was always the case.

The only good thing about Greek Week from my perspective was that I had nothing to do with it, but my contract required that I prepare food for three other major events: the Christmas party, a dinner to celebrate the installation of new officers in February, and the annual gathering of alumni Founders' Day in May. But some months into the job, I realized that my oldest son was graduating from college in New York on the same Saturday in May. A better mother would have had this date sealed in her brain before signing, but I was a good enough mother to attend and Bob arranged a catered barbecue, which the guys were fine with, as they were about most things. It was that easy attitude that got me through the first year, an attitude that could be problematic when applied to their own behavior, but when applied to *mine* was just fine by me.

Because I had no experience managing a professional kitchen, there were lots of mistakes, which the guys, if they noticed, overlooked. I learned that even if I had a walk-in refrigerator, which I did not for years, it made no sense to buy whole cases of some products. Thirty heads of celery doesn't sound outlandish until you find yourself trying to sneak it into muffins or come up with side dishes like Celery and Tofu Salad, tofu being another item you should just go to the grocery store and buy four, not *twenty-four,* pounds of at a time. Twenty-four heads of lettuce would still be at twelve by the time I had to toss it. A case of cornstarch had 4,032 teaspoons, an amount that unless you were cooking bad Chinese food every day of the week, you were never going to get through. I sometimes wondered why my food sales guy Kirk didn't try to save me, but I suppose it was hard to advise someone who looked at the lists of food ordered by other fraternity cooks and laughed.

Kirk had come to this job from a coffee background, which for some reason always made me question anything he said about food. Though I would later learn from him that one of their new reps had been a manager of a nail salon, which suddenly made Kirk seem like Escoffier. Food sales reps, I discovered, were not hired for culinary knowledge but like any other salesmen, I suppose, for their ability to hide what they really thought about the customer. He didn't say so exactly, but from the start, I sensed that Kirk regarded me as something of a challenge, with unrealistic ideas about what frat boys would eat and what was possible on a budget. So it probably seemed perfectly normal "for someone like you," as he often put it, to order whole boatloads of celery and tofu. And I guess for fear of showing my own self-doubts, I acted as if I knew exactly what I was doing even as I snuck fifty pounds of beets into places they didn't belong.

That first year several of the guys told me they'd grown up eating little more than Pop-Tarts and Kraft Dinners, yet they were surprisingly willing to go along with my frat food makeover—with some intransigent demands. Except for tomato, soups had to have at least a trace of meat. "But what's the main stuff?" one of the guys asked when I offered a silky butternut squash bisque. "Regular" salad met with tepid response, but you couldn't make enough Caesar. Carrot and (Get Rid of the Case of) Celery Stir-Fry, next to a Chinese pork dish, went completely untouched. But they were thrilled with fajitas and meatballs that didn't come out of a bag, and didn't think me crazy for squeezing ten pounds of fresh limes, even though I often had doubts about the lengths I would go to, to prove that I could. "Where's your green stuff?" I would have to prod some of them when I caught sight of a plate piled with browns and whites. Sometimes I would see them smelling and picking at something like they were dissecting a bug. But more often they were like Jake, looking apprehensively at a bowl of fruit and saying, "I've never eaten kiwi," before exclaiming seconds later, "I *love* kiwi!" And it was that kind of thing that assured me I hadn't failed.

It was at the end of that first year at the Alpha Sig House that my mother found a manila folder filled with recipes in my dad's handwriting. He had loved to cook as a way of recreating memorable experiences from his travels, as if making Paella Valenciana put you right back on the coast of Spain. And as I flipped through them, I remembered not just specific times he'd made the Crabmeat Imperial and the Coquilles St. Jacques, but times I'd been with him in various cities.

Some were written on notepaper and some on business let-
terhead and one was titled Darlene's Lamb Curry, which
wasn't really mine, but one that I'd referred him to. Tucked in
as well was a photocopied letter he'd written to me when I
was a freshman at the University of Michigan and it reminded
me of how really crappy that time in your life can be, how it
probably was now for a lot of my guys, and how much it matters to have someone want to hear you:

> Your letters are a real treat. We like to hear about your
> impressions of everything. Tell us about your food,
> how you get your laundry done, how far you have to
> walk to get to class, problems with people, the
> weather, problems with anything. We are interested in
> all of it.

I thought about that letter, and about all those awkward
and uncertain years after high school, when one of the guys
would plant himself on my kitchen stool and tell me about
the routine details of his day. And I reminded myself that he
wasn't telling me something I *needed* to know, or often even
wanted to know, but that it mattered to him that I was there
to listen. I had been insecure about all the professional knowledge I lacked when I started my own pledge year, all the technical information I didn't have, unaware that I had so much
else in me that mattered more.

SALAD DRESSINGS

Gallon tubs of weirdly gelatinous, metallic food service salad dressings were the norm at sororities and fraternities. Along with soups, these are some of the easiest, cheapest, and best items to prepare from scratch.

Homemade Ranch

Vary the proportions of the sour cream/mayo/buttermilk mixture depending on whether you want it to be richer (more mayo) or tangier (more sour cream and buttermilk).

½ **cup sour cream**
½ **cup mayonnaise**
¼ **cup buttermilk**
a little fresh lemon juice
garlic powder or fresh garlic, mashed with a little salt
    to form a paste (oddly, garlic powder makes it taste
    more "ranchy")
¼ **cup fresh herbs (chives and dill are great, but you**
    can use any fresh green herbs you happen to have)
salt and pepper

Stir everything together and adjust seasoning and herbs to taste.

Basic Vinaigrette

This is the one I can't believe anyone who calls himself a professional cook actually buys. I mean, seriously?

1 part vinegar (any kind)
3 parts olive oil

To this basic mixture you can add prepared mustard, which will make for a thicker dressing. Fresh herbs, garlic, salt, and black pepper can also be added.

Orange Balsamic Dressing

½ cup balsamic vinegar
zest of 1 orange
½ cup fresh orange juice
2 T. Dijon mustard
1 cup extra virgin olive oil
salt and black pepper

Combine the vinegar, orange zest, orange juice, and mustard in a food processor. Drizzle in the olive oil. Add salt and pepper to taste.

Sherry Mustard Vinaigrette

1 shallot, finely minced
1 T. Dijon mustard
1 tsp. black pepper
½ tsp. salt
½ cup sherry vinegar

1½ cups olive oil
2 T. chopped tarragon

Whisk together the shallot, mustard, pepper, salt, and sherry vinegar. Drizzle in the oil, whisking until incorporated. Stir in the tarragon.

Caesar Dressing

I started using shredded kale instead of romaine lettuce for my Caesar salads both because it was an easy way to incorporate a really healthy green and because you can dress kale hours (even a day) ahead of time and it only improves, rather than wilting.

FOR 2 CUPS:

1 oz. anchovy fillets
2 cloves garlic
1 egg
1 T. fresh lemon juice
¾ cup olive oil
⅓ cup canola oil
½ tsp. black pepper
½ cup fresh lemon juice
1 tsp. Worcestershire sauce
¾ cup grated Parmesan

Puree the anchovies, garlic, egg, and lemon juice in a food processor. Slowly pour in the oils until you have a mayonnaise. Stir in the black pepper, the additional lemon juice, the Worcestershire sauce, and the Parmesan cheese.

The Right Fit

I doubt very seriously whether anyone will hire me . . .
Employers sense in me a denial of their values.
—IGNATIUS REILLY IN *A CONFEDERACY OF DUNCES*,
  JOHN KENNEDY TOOLE

I appreciate everything you do for us. Please, please take care
of yourself before coming to work. We can manage . . . somehow.
—TEXT FROM COREY

All through the years, there were a precious few guys in the House who understood how a really very small word or gesture could instantly turn my vile mood around. My head could be ready to explode and then there would be that one little expression of gratitude that would smother the inferno. Corey was one of them. A junior at the time he sent this text and the treasurer, he'd been one of my favorites since his pledge year when I remarked online that "he's very adorable, he will make a fabulous husband and his mom should be so proud." And he didn't hate me for the public gushing. He was one of the smartest and most thoughtful guys I'd encountered and when he was near graduation he sympathized with me, sharing his view that "this place really wears you down after a while," without taking any credit for being one of those people who made it very much less wearing.

The texted words appeared on my phone just after a nurse had bandaged my severely cut hand, cut with poultry shears I was stupidly using to lop off the ends of some flowers they'd given me and not while butchering chickens. "You'll get lots of sympathy from your guys when they see this," she had said. And I laughed that I wouldn't, that they'd take one look at that and wonder who was going to cook. And then the text came. I had smiled when I saw his message; it was one of many moments, along with the sounds of opera singing filling the main floor and the giddy group adoption of a kitten that challenged a simple narrative about working in a frat house. I would tell people who assumed that it must be a very sexist and hostile environment that I had never felt more empowered and respected in any other workplace.

When I took the job, it didn't seem especially strange to me to be surrounded by men. I'd grown up sandwiched between two brothers, I had sons, and I'd been working in the food industry for several years, an oddly male-dominated field. My apprehensions weren't about their sex. What had seemed to be my problem at other jobs, even though many were as heavily populated with men as the food world, wasn't my lack of a penis; it was my lack of enthusiasm and a self-attached muzzle. And it wasn't only men who had a problem with that;

women, too, came down hard on employees who were just saying out loud what everyone else was thinking.

Before the food-related jobs I'd had in the years immediately preceding my time at the fraternity, there'd been a series of positions for which I was as ill suited as I was for the one with the Robertsons. I worked sporadically while my kids were growing up, taking jobs I was overqualified for, always a mistake, but especially when you're someone who feels compelled to show your employer just how overqualified you are by being terrible at the lousy job the company hired you to fill. In the early years, my husband was a military officer so we moved frequently, making it difficult for me to establish any kind of career with an English degree and no experience. But when our second child, Simon, was old enough for day care, I made a trial run at finding work that satisfied.

The first of those efforts was as a receptionist at a human resources management company, a position the hiring manager was resistant to offer me, rightly assessing that someone with a college education might have a low tolerance for the long periods of boredom broken by the stress of multiple calls at once, and the tedium of a job that never changed from one day to the next. Forever. I persuaded her to take a chance on me in the mistaken belief that answering phones would somehow reveal my superior organizational and communication skills.

It didn't help that I had no skill at all in communicating with angry asshole clients who invariably called when the person they were angry at was off enjoying an expense-account lunch. Chaucer and Shakespeare had ill prepared me for keeping track of who was on hold and pushing the button that would send them to their desired destination instead of to the sound of a dial tone. I never did get past the reception desk, realizing later what a mistake it is to become thoroughly competent at a job that you hate but that the organization considers vital and hard to fill with someone who doesn't file her nails while the lights of incoming calls are furiously flashing.

I decided that it was my lack of postgraduate education or specific technical training that was holding me back. So several years later, after serving on a jury while we were living in Colorado, I took a seven-month paralegal course. I'd been called to jury duty in federal court in Denver just before the Oklahoma City bombing trial of Terry Nichols and waited in the halls with all the other prospective jurors before being assigned—not to Nichols, but to a wrongful arrest civil suit against a Denver police officer.

Even without the glamour of the more sensational trial going on in the same building, I loved the courtroom atmosphere and so enjoyed arguing my points with the other jurors that I held out on a verdict on Friday, sincerely believing that I was right, forcing us all to return the following Monday when I knew that they would all come to see things my way. It was thrilling when they did, likely because they were enjoying this duty less than I was, most of them having actual bill-paying jobs to get back to and just wanting to go home. But what I didn't realize until I'd finished my $7,000 course was that few paralegals ever see a courtroom; even the ones who get the relatively few jobs in criminal law spend their time doing the necessary but tedious tasks in windowless offices that their bosses paid massively higher tuition to avoid. Most of my classmates took internships with large firms and government agencies where they intended to find permanent work, but I wanted a few weeks of denial and took an unpaid internship with the public defender's office, where I knew I had little chance of remaining long-term without a law degree.

I was assigned to a gritty female attorney preparing for a rape trial and managing various other cases, and spent my days sifting through thousands of pages of evidence that read like a mystery novel, calling witnesses, conducting jail interviews with an armed guard standing on the other side of the glass for my protection from our mostly clinically insane defendants, and attending the trial that ended with our client being removed in handcuffs. It was heady stuff, but when it was over I accepted a job working with a corporate attorney on mergers and acquisitions at a multistate veterinary management company.

And that was the horrible truth they hid from us at paralegal school; most of the paid jobs involved working for inhouse counsel at private companies preparing contracts and filing applications with the secretary of state. They didn't involve blood trails and DNA and so, disillusioned, I became one of those poisonous problem employees who refuses to clap at motivational morning meetings and infects everyone in the break room with her sarcastic rewriting of the company mission statement.

When I left after less than three years, I decided that it wasn't specific training I lacked but passion for the job, which is what led me to a mass-hiring event at the newly opened gourmet grocery store Central Market in Plano, Texas. We had moved there the year before and the managers were seeking food-obsessed people, putting potential hires through a series of tests set up in various rooms. I excelled at the ones identifying ingredients by sight and taste, but was less successful when handed a product and told to create an on-the-spot sales pitch. And I wasn't enthusiastic about the test requiring us to put together a collage using arts and crafts materials and school glue, and to name our creation, not that it wasn't as fun as being back in kindergarten, but because I thought it wasn't really about food and was instead a psychological test. I'd already failed one of those with Whole Foods, and while I have no confirmation as to why I've always suspected it was because they determined I was a liar when I answered "disagree" to the question "there are some people I really can't stand."

The recruitment team hired me on the strength of my food knowledge and in spite of my lack of sales ability, not to mention my complete inability to control my facial expressions and body language, which betrayed the fact there really are people I can't stand. They assigned me to the Chef's Case, the glass-front display of prepared foods that was not where I wanted to be. I had specified my preference as kitchen work, joining the twenty other chefs and cooks, but instead I was out on the floor required to smile until my face hurt and sell food that was prepared, not with the wonderful and expensive fresh ingredients available for purchase in the rest of the store, but with a completely separate shipment of items for kitchen use.

More than my lack of enthusiasm for sales, I suffered from a lack of enthusiasm for serving customers who make you dig through the twice-baked potatoes to get exactly the one they wanted. I received a transfer to the kitchen when management determined that even if I wasn't technically qualified, I could do less harm in the back of house. But even with a woman in the role of executive chef overseeing the assignment of roles, I was stuck in the catering kitchen, where I had no decision-making powers, even tiny ones like in which direction to place the baby carrots. And so I left that job for the even more oppressive one of catering to the Robertsons.

By the time I took the job with the Alpha Sigs, I had been in the food industry for four years and yet had never dealt with suppliers, or been responsible for purchasing equipment, or been included on guest lists for trade shows and customer appreciation events. So all the things that came with the Alpha Sig job had previously been reserved for the "real" chefs that I reported to. The contract Bob and Alex presented to me at Starbucks had the words "food services manager" at the top, which was much better than "chef" because it gave me the power to run the place "like your own restaurant," as Bob put it. He arranged for business cards that I could hand to vendors who poked their heads into the kitchen asking me who they needed to talk to. And he told Josh, the first vice president boss I had upon hiring, that his only real job was to "keep Darlene happy."

My son Simon inherited my impulsive and sometimes unfiltered personality and his teachers found him as difficult as my former employers had found me, often calling Phil and me into meetings to discuss what to do with our child who refused to conform. He was both "too aggressive" and "too sensitive," he was "too talkative," and he had "too many girlfriends," whatever that was supposed to mean. It was agonizing for a mother to have her child continually judged and when I told a friend that everyone had ideas about a makeover for him, she said, "I have an idea. How about we let Simon be Simon." And over time there were teachers and professors who did just that and he thrived. That's how it was for me when I found my way to the Alpha Sig House after years of disillusionment and failure to settle on one right thing.

So it wasn't just that my guys gave me total menu control and the authority to make decisions affecting my work that kept me there. It was that they let me be myself, even when that self could be just a little too much. They might be frat boys, singing anachronistically sexist songs to sorority girls with lines like "who has the right to kiss you goodnight?" and getting slightly obnoxious at restaurants on the Ave and at Sounders games, but there was nowhere I could think of that was more genuine and loving and supportive than in that House.

When alumnus Alex, who'd interviewed me for the Alpha Sig job while he was a junior, heard that I was planning to leave one year, he laughed it off with the question I kept asking myself: "Where is she going to go? Where else can she do whatever the hell she wants and talk shit about her customers?" There wasn't anywhere else like that and I knew it well.

5

More Than Food

Texts between Badley and me:

> **B:** My stomach hurts from the sorority food!!!
>
> **D:** Good then you will appreciate me.
>
> **B:** I always appreciate you! I feel hella sick now! You should make chicken noodle tomorrow.
>
> **D:** Isn't there a weed that's supposed to help with nausea?
>
> **B:** Yeah, but chicken soup would be better.

By the end of my first year there were already signs that I was inextricably bound to the Alpha Sig House. Bob, who was generally suspicious of anyone who wasn't part of the fraternity working on the property, and would have preferred to have every service provider, the fire department, and the health inspector be Alpha Sigs, referred to me as part of The Family. And the guys began to text me so often that

I had to move my phone out of the bedroom to avoid 3:00 A.M. party invitations or menu requests they'd suddenly felt compelled to share. When one of them sent an invitation to their latest holiday gathering, I was sitting at home with Phil watching a movie and texted back that I wasn't interested because I was having "hot Halloween sex with my husband," a response that Phil reacted to with a wary, "You can't say that." The recipient then shared it with everyone in the House and everyone in the House shared it with everyone they knew, parents included.

But as fun and transformative as the first year had been for all of us, inevitably the honeymoon was over and the incoming freshmen had no appreciation for what the food had been like in prior years. Instead of focusing on the Newmans and the Badleys who brightened my days, I spent this whole year missing the good that was right in front of me.

When I looked back at my time at the fraternity, I vividly remembered the first year and the third through the sixth, but I could recall nothing at all about the second year. And then it all came back to me in pieces like one of those nightmares you suddenly remember the next day that makes you illogically furious with your husband because in your dream he slept with Angelina Jolie who was somehow the mother of your first-born who she gave up for adoption because he looked just like you. Except in this case, the second year really did happen, and with few exceptions there had been no bonding between that pledge class and me. But I did remember this without any trouble: At the end of the second year, I quit. Or at least I meant to. And then something happened that changed everything.

It all began with great hope and anticipation. I had heard

that many Greek system cooks were attracted to the job for the sole purpose of fraudulently collecting unemployment insurance during the summer. But I wanted to be at the House and instead of enjoying my time off like a normal person, I was there for weeks that first summer, painting bright white over the grease-and-smoke-yellow kitchen walls, a shade I was pretty sure no one had picked from swatches at Home Depot. There was a paper plate painted onto the wall and food scraps, too, a sure sign that the last laborer had been one of those pledges who does just exactly what he's told and not one thing more. I left the paper plate because it proclaimed a sort of defiance that I liked and it was a conversation piece for adult visitors who would look at the round shape and ridges and slowly realize that *a paper plate is painted onto the wall.* But the crusty food had to go. I scrubbed and painted the shelving in my pantry, turned my kitchen door black, and installed magnetic strips for attaching photographs of the customers I'd already started to call my guys. And I planned months of menus that I knew I would toss in favor of my impulsive style of cooking, but somehow the planning warmed me the way scrubbing baseboards warms a pregnant woman as she creates a clean little nest for her newborn. I did all of this in the summer because I wanted to start the new school year just exactly so.

I had spent the first year trying to undo the worst examples of frat life, food being the only thing I really had any control over. And in the summer, besides working on my kitchen, I cleaned the "women's" bathroom and installed new hardware so the toilet paper would live at least a foot off the wet floor and paper towels would live in a dispenser instead of in the often-pukey sinks. I actually believed that going the further step of placing fresh flowers and scented candles in the room would set an example and a tone that they would adopt throughout the House. I actually seriously *believed* this. It was not long before the room reverted to its former state and I resigned myself to BYOTP. I kept a roll in the kitchen, explaining it to visitors who thought it was a weird addition to the spice rack.

I made another attempt to hire outside kitchen help, once again resisting Bob's preference for keeping it internal, and started the year off with James, a directionless high school graduate who'd taken some vocational culinary classes. He had bleached-white hair and a lip piercing that I didn't have a problem with, except I sometimes couldn't focus on what he was saying because I was too distracted by the thing he'd done to his face on purpose. I hired him because he made me laugh, a weakness of mine that explains why I loved certain guys in the House even if they lacked a single quality I could cite in an HR background check—"he's hilarious" not being something most employers rate as a plus. James also had knife skills and expressed an interest in going on to culinary school, so I adopted him, thinking I could be a mentor of hard work and dedication, which proved about as effective as my attempts at beautifying the House by example.

It started almost immediately with lateness and messages about traffic delays, and in less than the three-month probation period, I lost my kitchen help, finding that tanned, tattooed, and pierced James's comedic skills did not make up for a lack of certain basics like showing up regularly and on time, not answering sixty texts a day, and staying in the kitchen for more than thirty minutes at a stretch. I finally had to accept that James, like 99 percent of the people employed in this field, was a pothead after about the fiftieth time of finding him standing in the shrubbery without a good explanation. It was harder to count on someone who constantly disappointed than to just go it alone, and so when he was a no-show, no-call for the third time in less than three months, I texted him the breakup news that "Alpha Sigma Phi has terminated your employment for cause," resisting the temptation to add "you worthless idiot."

I came to think of this as the horrible year for good reason, but apart from the disappointment of James, there was every sign at the outset that it should have gone smoothly, the way welcoming my second baby had been effortless after the steep learning curve of the first. For one thing, and a really major thing, Perry became vice president, making him my boss. He was already a junior when I joined the House, a skinny blond with a goofy grin that I couldn't help return. And as the child of a struggling single mom, he took the path of fierce self-sufficiency over victimhood, paying his own way through school, both unspoiled and unassuming. Unlike his predecessor in the role of vice president, Perry was almost my twin in temperament, deploring laziness and messes and refusing to just live with it. I'm sure he must have had failings, but I never saw any. The same way others, without uttering a word, could suck the life right out of me, Perry could energize me just by showing up. I caught him one day sweeping up hundreds of sunflower seeds strewn on the back stairs and when I asked why he was taking care of something he wasn't responsible for, he responded that he couldn't live like that and he wasn't going to wait for someone else to suddenly make the world livable for him.

"Morning, Darlene!" he'd call from upstairs each day

when he heard me unlocking the kitchen door. And that one simple thing made me overlook his being the pickiest eater I've ever encountered, someone whose ideal meal was a grilled chicken breast with a side of grilled chicken breast, that person who would pick the tiny pieces of mushroom out of the chicken pie and scrape the garlic-herb crust off the pork loin. He was a constant presence in the kitchen and a reliable source of gossip and information, visiting every morning before class to let me know about any stories I might be reading in the paper later, or, more typically, harmless but funny things that I was never going to hear about otherwise. But even Perry with his goofy smile and unwavering support couldn't make up for the dulling of appreciation that I guess was normal after the total lovefest of the previous year.

My first clue that this was going to be a different sort of year than the previous one, when beaming young men received me like an angel, was the sight of twenty pledges sitting at a table on the first day of Work Week, waiting to be served coffee. After my third trip past them without delivering, they began to shift irritably, remarking at the need for someone to clean up the place. Pledge Mitchell, looking like most of the rest, dressed for a yacht outing rather than a floor scrubbing, poked his head into the kitchen, where I was working on lunch, and asked innocently enough, yawning and rubbing his eyes, when breakfast was coming out. And I explained how things work around here, asking if he needed me to pour milk on his cereal, which is the sort of response that explains why most of that group of freshmen regarded me as "intimidating."

It was only in fact a few new pledges who seemed to think my name was either Cook or Maid, but they had such a powerful effect on my morale that I lumped them all together and was surprised years later when I realized that Stoecker had been in that class. Stoecker was someone who once suggested that I take him on a trip to Europe as my companion in a way that made me blush and was so genuinely charming that I refused to see a single fault in him, much to the annoyance of other guys who picked out shortcomings they knew I'd disapprove of, like his inability to get out of bed before noon and class attendance that put him on the "five-year degree plan." I had forgotten that it was that year when he first stood in my kitchen, arms loaded with ground deer and antelope from his dad's hunting trip, melting my heart when he grinned that he'd stuck a few steaks in there just for me. And Stoecker wasn't alone. But what I had chosen to focus on instead were the pledges who scrawled SANDWICHES, SANDWICHES, SANDWICHES across my lunch menu one week, a protest followed up a few days later with YOU SHOULD TRY HARDER, posted on the fridge.

I would say that I didn't care what anyone thought, especially the tough customers who dominated that pledge class, but the truth is that I was obsessed with pleasing and proving and impressing. I was striving to be a different kind of frat cook and I was determined to demonstrate that every chance I got. Especially when I knew that anyone from the food industry was coming by, I felt compelled to ensure that chicken bones were simmering on the stove and that I was hand-forming meatballs or trimming pork tenderloins, anything to show off, like that know-it-all kid in class who can't keep her hand out of the air. So when Rod from our main food supplier was making his first sales call of the year during lunch, I decided the menu would be Crab and Corn Bisque that day. And precooked crab wasn't enough; it had to be *live* crab.

Newman had been asking for a boiled crab dinner, an

impractical request for sixty people. But soup was doable and Newman helped with the cooking, dropping them into the water for me. It was a task I felt comfortable assuming when one or two creatures were concerned, but I illogically felt like a mass murderer when it was a dozen. He helped with the cleaning and picking, too. With the skill and diligence of someone who'd done this before, he asked if I wanted to keep the fat rather than needing to ask what that thick yellow stuff was. And when I was finished with the stock from the shells and the vegetable chopping, and the corn scraping (because of course it had to be fresh from the cob and not frozen kernels), and the addition of cream and sherry and crabmeat, it was delicious enough to make up for the absurdity of overachieving on the show-off scale by a factor of ten. But it did not go into regular lunch rotation. Some of what made that year hard for me was *me*. I was becoming like the women relatives I remembered from my childhood who would spend all day making Thanksgiving dinner and then get mad at the diners who were done in ten minutes, not nearly as thankful as they goddamn well should have been.

Rod helped himself to a large bowl of the bisque, remarking that he carried the same soup, frozen and vacuum-sealed by Ivar's restaurant, and that it didn't require the services of a cook's pet like Newman. Without kids of his own, Rod took a welcome interest in the guys, learning their names and asking about their majors and jobs, often pointing them in the direction of sales as a career. And since many of them were in business school at the time, they took note of his offer to contact him after graduation, even Perry, who'd seen enough of my interactions with salespeople to remark, "But then I'd have to deal with *her*," while looking straight in my direction. And even though he'd said it teasingly and everyone gathered in the kitchen had laughed—a little too long—it was obvious that the work environment was wearing on me. Most of those guys were not asking me to try harder and were happy with the simpler things and just wanted me to lighten up.

But it was hard to do that when you were trying to be the Martha Stewart of the fraternity kitchen and your customers were not getting with the program. Instead they were leaving leftover food sitting out overnight to be tossed into the trash the next morning, attacking the lunch table like hyenas, and asking for Tater Tot Casserole the night you spent four hours on the components for Veal Sentino. I started to wonder if this grand experiment was more for me than them; I'd become so consumed with putting out great food that I'd forgotten the part about making people happy.

So in May I interviewed for a restaurant position, having decided that any more than two years with "fraternity" on my résumé was a liability. I also began to feel that I was becoming too much a part of their world, that Stockholm syndrome was taking over my good sense. "Have you ever been inside a frat house?" was my response to anyone questioning why I wanted out of one. But it wasn't enough for the executive chef conducting the interview, who seemed to like me less the more I talked about the job I wanted to leave. "So, you work Monday to Friday, no nights or weekends or holidays, basically run your own show, and you make more than I do?" he asked, obviously failing to grasp what my problem was.

And when I thought about it, I saw his point. But really, it wasn't the sweet schedule and better-than-average pay in a dismally low-wage field that had kept me there. It was that I was certain that most of my customers were a whole lot more fun than his. I loved that when I presented them with a hundred things I'd worked hard at, most weren't, like my last employer, pointing out the one tiny mistake, that they didn't even notice the mistakes, that I could tell them the ever-so-slightly-burned sweet potatoes were supposed to be that way for a tinge of balancing bitterness, and they were just completely cool with that.

Still I was bone-weary and went to the House on the first day of summer break to clean up my kitchen for the last time. I had not shared this intention with Bob or any of the guys and had in fact signed a contract for the following year—as yet unable to make a public and final break. I knew I could wait a couple of weeks until I'd found another job and that they would still have all summer to interview. Phil, who'd always been supportive, was nevertheless blunt in his assessment that "I'd have quit a long time ago." And then I thought about my own interview, how Bob had told me they wanted someone who would stay for years and be part of The Family, and the guilt over both the leaving and the lying was terrible. But I wanted a real job, the kind I could tell people about at my husband's business dinners without feeling like I'd just announced my profession as stripper or crack dealer. I didn't see that what I was doing was as real as any other occupation, and I'd forgotten about all the respectable jobs I'd had before this one that I hated. I was about to get my perspective back, along with a reminder that my work was about more than food.

SOUPS

A few easy homemade soups that don't require a dozen live crabs, four hours, and an assistant.

Chicken Tortellini Soup

I'm not sure how much of this I'd have to make to satisfy the demand. I finally quit trying at 4 1/2 gallons. I made this often, but especially during finals week or when they needed something comforting and I sensed that my faro salads and sautéed kale just weren't doing it for them.

FOR APPROXIMATELY 1 GALLON:

1 large onion, chopped
4 or 5 stalks of celery, chopped
6 T. butter
6 T. flour
1 T. salt
1 1/2 tsp. black pepper
1 1/2 tsp. dried thyme
1 1/2 tsp. cayenne pepper
8 cups chicken stock
3 1/2 cups heavy cream
2 lbs. chicken, cooked and shredded
1–1 1/2 lbs. frozen cheese tortellini
1/2 cup chopped fresh Italian parsley

Sauté the onion and celery in the butter. Stir in the flour and the seasonings and cook for a couple of minutes. Gradually add the stock and simmer until thickened. Add the cream and continue to cook until hot, seasoning as necessary. Add the remaining ingredients and cook until thoroughly hot.

Italian Sausage and White Bean Soup

Hearty, healthy, and freezes well. And like a lot of soups, this is better after a day or two.

FOR APPROXIMATELY 2 GALLONS:

3 medium onions, chopped
¼ cup olive oil
15 cloves garlic, chopped
1½ tsp. salt
½ lb. celery, chopped
4 oz. (about ½ cup) tomato paste
1¼ lbs. dry white beans, cooked
4 lbs. Italian sausage, cooked and diced
6 cups chopped tomatoes
8 cups chicken stock
1 T. crushed red pepper
1½ T. dried basil
1½ T. dried oregano
2 oz. sun-dried tomatoes, diced
fresh basil, thinly sliced just before adding to soup

Sauté the onion in the olive oil until softened. Add the garlic and continue cooking for a minute or two before adding the salt and celery. When the celery softens slightly, add the tomato paste and cook for a couple of minutes until it darkens slightly. Puree ⅓ of the beans in a food processor and add them to the pot along with the whole beans, the sausage, tomatoes, chicken stock, spices, and sun-dried tomatoes. Simmer until hot and thickened slightly. Season to taste and add the fresh basil just before serving.

Chicken Tortilla Soup

To make this vegetarian, use vegetable stock and replace the chicken with black beans or garbanzo beans.

FOR ABOUT 10 CUPS:

3 corn tortillas, cut into thin strips
vegetable oil for frying
½ onion, chopped
1 T. olive oil
2 cloves garlic
1½ tsp. smoked paprika
1½ tsp. ground cumin
1½ tsp. ground coriander
1 tsp. chipotle chili powder
¼ tsp. cayenne
1½ tsp. smoked chipotle Tabasco
4 cups chicken broth
1½ cups crushed tomatoes
1 bay leaf
1½ tsp. salt
1 lb. boneless, skinless chicken breast or thighs
1½ cups hominy (optional, but it gives a nice flavor
    and texture)
1 T. fresh lime juice
2 T. chopped cilantro

Fry the tortilla strips in vegetable oil, drain on a paper towel, and add salt to taste. Set aside. (You can bake these at 350 degrees until crisp for a lighter version.) Sauté the onions in olive oil until golden. Add the garlic and cook a couple of minutes. Add the spices and let toast slightly by cooking a couple of minutes, stirring. Add the remaining ingredients except the hominy, lime juice, and cilantro and simmer until the chicken is cooked through. Add the hominy and simmer a few minutes longer. Remove the bay leaf. Stir in the fresh cilantro. Serve topped with the tortilla strips.

6

Tread Carefully

It was one of those glorious, sunny Seattle June mornings when I went to the House to clean up for what I thought was the last time. It was Perry's graduation day, the only senior in the House finishing on time, and I had watched with resignation as he'd headed off to an interview with Rod for a potential food sales job, late, unshaven, and tieless, reminding myself as I often did with the guys that I was not his mom. I had promised to attend a celebration later in the afternoon at the home of his girlfriend, Leah. But when I got to the kitchen door, he was sitting on the stairs, ashen, with alumnus and Corporate Board president Chris standing nearby. And when they didn't return my smile or my hello and didn't ask why I was even there on a Saturday morning, I knew I was not going to be doing any kitchen cleaning that day. My first thought was that something had happened to Bob, whom I'd had trouble reaching for days. "Kevin MacDonald," Chris began, and I knew what was coming and suddenly pictured the last time I'd seen Kevin, poking his head into the kitchen, attempting to drag me out of a bad mood, which had become my usual mood lately. "Come on, Darlene, it's *funny*," he'd said after telling me about his antics the night before.

On Friday, the last day of final exams, Kevin had dialed his mother late at night, presumably accidentally, leaving no message. Sophomore Brian, who'd worked with me in the kitchen during his pledge year, my first year, had been the last person known to have seen Kevin sitting alone in the dark in the dining hall, he later told me. Shortly afterward, he had fallen from his third-story bedroom window onto the concrete below, creating enough commotion to send Brian and freshman Stoecker rushing to his side, where the sounds of his desperate attempts to breathe created a hope that we all held on to for many hours. When Chris gave me the news, I spent some time in the kitchen, unsure where I should be. There were a couple of guys so amazingly callous that they went on about their day as usual, one complaining to me that all of the fuss the night before had interrupted his rare score with a girl he'd been pursuing. And there were a couple so traumatized by having been first at the scene that they couldn't speak. And so I went where I thought I should be and found at least twenty of my guys sitting against a wall in the ICU, their heads between their knees, one of them sobbing so uncontrollably that a pool had formed at his feet. And it was such a scene of raw emotion that I wondered if I should be there, if they even wanted me there after the way I'd been all year, until, one by one, they reached out to me for the hug they were unable to give each other.

In the room where Kevin lay, his head so swollen he was almost unrecognizable, a half-circle of guys parted to make room for me, Newman and Dan locking arms around my waist. We stood there silently watching the family at the bed and then Kevin's mom approached and began to ask if I was who she thought, and I stammered my name and added stupidly that "I love your son," glad that at least I had gotten the words out in the present tense, although we all knew where this was going. When I walked out of the room, hospital employees for whom this was just another workday were chattering amiably, laughing casually around a workstation, and I thought about other times in my life in hospitals when the world had changed horribly for me, but impossibly went on as usual for everyone else.

As I left the building, my food sales guy Kirk called to tell me he'd heard the news, that he'd known instantly which house it was when he'd seen the TV footage. "I know what those guys are to you." Back at the House, Perry descended the stairs in cap and gown, alone, and I couldn't think of any words to make it an easier day for him. Brian, who'd been last to see Kevin before the fall and then was the first at his side, sat in the living room shaking and sweating. Stoecker, who'd been too distraught to make his way to the hospital, stood in the dining hall looking disoriented. I handed him a mop and told him we needed to clean up, that people would be coming, but it was really just to give him something to do. Badley stood in the kitchen expressionless and told me that he didn't know how he was supposed to feel. "I never had anyone die before," he told me. And the next few days were like that, answering impossible questions and assigning jobs to guys who needed help putting one foot in front of the other.

Before I left for the night, I made Coconut Blondies, a recipe I pulled from that month's *Gourmet*. Chris, who'd given me the news, had been in and out of the House, another adult to keep things together, and I told him that I didn't know what I could do, that I only knew to cook, and I had that magazine with me and made that particular recipe for no other reason than it was staring at me. I didn't think about whether they would like coconut or prefer chocolate to butterscotch. I thought about nothing at all as I watched the brown sugar melt into the butter and whisked in the eggs one by one and smelled the vanilla and the pecans toasting just until fragrant. I left them outside the kitchen with a note that I wanted to give them some privacy but that I didn't live far away, and that it was okay to call or text. I heard later that they'd gathered with UW counselors to talk about their feelings and the first thing they had done was to eat those bar cookies, wordlessly.

Thank you for everything today.

Thanks for the note. It was really nice. We ate all of the treats last night. Your support really helped and we noticed. Thank you again.

The next morning, before realizing the absurdity of it, I remarked to Bob that we would need to plan the service, the sense of family here being so intense that I had forgotten our place and that he was not ours to plan for. "If I ever thought this was just a job, I know differently now," I added in an email to Rod requesting an unscheduled delivery for the following Wednesday, the guys having decided to hold a dinner at the House before a public vigil on Thursday. Rod had seen the sensational reporting on TV, the ominous voice-over of a reporter stating that "questions remain" as the camera panned around the front of the House, up to Kevin's third-floor window. Rod had called to see how I was, a welcome outreach from a second person who knew my guys as something other than generic frat boys. When I'd interviewed for the restaurant job, I'd asked him for a reference, and he'd sent me the irritatingly insightful message: "I don't know why you keep looking when you know you don't want to leave."

And now there was no question of me leaving, because while there hadn't been time to be much of a part of Kevin's life, I looked around at everyone still at the House and knew it could have been any one of them. There was no question that even though it was summer and my contract had ended, I would be there Monday morning, making omelets for whichever guys were around and meals for the family. Those days were the beginning of my kitchen as a place where several guys at a time would hang out for more than something to eat, often for nothing to eat. We were there laughing about some remembered piece of K-Mac history when Badley told me that Kevin's mom was in the study and that no one knew what to do. When I told them that we would all go see her, several of them expressed doubts about what to say. "It doesn't matter what you say," I told them. "She won't even hear you." And as we approached her, she was smiling and spoke so casually about the cremation that it was obvious she was a complete wreck and we were really sure she wasn't hearing anything at all.

Where were you today ... I made omelets for everyone ... take care.

I'm with Matt ... It's hard for us to be back at the house right now. Thanks for coming by, I thank you for being there for the guys.

By Thursday morning, five days after the fall, I'd absorbed so much of everyone else's grief that I was bursting with it and sat in a therapist's office for the first time in my life. But in choosing the first person who could see me right away, I had made the unfortunate choice of a fraternity-averse psychoanalyst, a fact I gathered too late as she made broad generalizations about the community a few blocks from her office. And rather than listen, she seemed more interested in telling me about her own experiences with the suicides of loved ones, seemingly a lot of lost loved ones, so that I began to feel annoyed, which made me feel guilty. "But I don't think he killed himself," I told her, before listening to more of her stories and deciding that I couldn't help her.

In the following days, Perry and I went over and over that night, trying to put together what we knew and fill in what we didn't. We talked about Brian's story of seeing Kevin sitting in the darkened dining hall, and we wondered how it was that the flower box at his window was undisturbed. We asked a hundred questions, as if by talking it through we could figure it all out. Almost immediately, insurance people were huddled at the House and as I walked past them in the living room one day, I was startled when the woman in the group asked me what I thought had happened.

By then I'd heard several scenarios and as they all looked at me expectantly I said, "None of it makes sense." And I got the feeling that they thought so, too, but that what they thought and what they argued in reports for the inevitable lawsuit were not necessarily the same thing. His room had been left untouched for the investigators, and I went up there, thinking that I could look at the scene and understand it. The window was open, the beds unmade. And at the base of the sliding ladder to his bunk, the legs were wedged into two of his large sneakers, holding it steady. So it hadn't slid dangerously, as one theory went. And we would probably never know the real story.

But plenty of people who knew nothing thought they had the answers and in the absence of facts, the media and school officials and people walking by on the street pointing up at the House just made stuff up. Newman did most of the actual talking to the press, at one point letting TV reporters in the House have a good look around before Nationals put a stop to it and a sign went on the front door letting the curious know that we would issue a press release and requesting privacy for now. It was also Newman who did most of the vigil planning. He chose photos and music and decided who would speak. Bob taught the guys the traditional mourning rituals: the candles in the shape of the symbol for Omega, the incantations, the sort of stuff that I'd called hocus-pocus when it was part of Initiation Week but that I was suddenly glad to see giving structure and a sense of dignity to what could so easily turn into an embarrassing spectacle.

Please be here Thursday for dinner and vigil. We all need you.

For brothers only, I cooked a meal, the same pot roast I had brought to the House for my interview, and alumni and current residents ate with just as much hunger, only now it was welcome in a different way. Some of Kevin's high school friends spoke that night and then his fraternity brothers. And there was an obvious distance between the two, as if each side were claiming Kevin as its own.

Among the music Newman had chosen was Big IZ's "Over

the Rainbow," which Kevin either loved or loved inflicting on his brothers. It was ringing out with incongruous cheerfulness as the ceremony ended and I found the recently graduated Perry looking as if he were about to crumble into a thousand pieces after holding it together for a week that was supposed to be a happy new chapter in his life. It was ages before I could bear to read the comments the guys had written on a canvas set up to record their thoughts, and along with the many "I love you's" there was one that seemed to hold a private memory of happier times: "You were worth every moment we waited to make you our Brother."

The vigil was what a memorial should be and all the more poignant for having been put together in a few days by guys who just a week earlier had done little more than plan beer-pong tournaments. But the funeral was horrible. We sat together as a team, several rows of dark-suited young men and Hilary, the sorority girlfriend of Dan, and Bob, and me with my husband. Half the rest in attendance, unknown to us and unrelated to our group, wore shorts and tank tops like they'd wandered in from a pool party. Kevin's mom, too stricken to speak, wrote her thoughts for a relative to read, thoughts that centered on her son's love of learning. And then the minister—who had not known the family, and stared straight at my guys—spoke of the evil of young men seeking knowledge and warned of their certain path to hell, which is presumably where Kevin had gone since just minutes before his mom had put him squarely in the camp of the learned. But the guys stared straight ahead and showed no reaction, and we all left feeling more depressed than ever. So I could understand that after a week of respectful sobriety, they wanted nothing more that night than to screw it all and get wasted.

That whole week while the guys hung out in the kitchen helping make omelets and sandwiches and meals for the family, Fionn Regan's *The End of History* played on an endless loop, all of us too absorbed in work and conversation and our private thoughts to change the album. And not because the lyrics have any relevance at all, but to this day, I can't hear the song "Be Good or Be Gone" without remembering how it felt to be in that kitchen, everyone as normal as they could be, comfortable about laughing as well as crying, relieved to be in a place where they didn't have to behave in any particular way.

Hey Darlene I just ate the dinner you brought by. Everything was really good. Thank you for doing that for Kevin's family.

Because I didn't want to leave them alone for months, I spent every Monday that summer making dinners that the twenty or so guys who were living in could enjoy with anyone who wanted to join them. I knew they'd appreciate it, but it was also a selfish thing, cooking for so relatively few people that I could shop the farmers' market and prepare the kinds of meals too complicated for large numbers. I had choices in the summer that I didn't during the school year, when the limited supply of fresh seasonal produce restricted me to mostly beets, Brussels sprouts, and potatoes.

Since I was there in the summer, I saw what is usually carried out in my absence: rush and the steady pledge-signing of new freshmen who would have no personal knowledge of our loss or the intense bonding among some of us that followed it. Grayson, one of that year's pledges, was part of the recruitment effort, a tough job after all the negative press attention. I wanted to sympathize when I saw him trying hard to invent new marketing angles, but he had the annoying habit of walking right past me when he gave tours to rushees. "Here is the TV room," he'd say, pointing to the room with a TV in it, "and here's the back door," pointing to the back door. But he said not a word about the woman in between who was filling the House with the kind of promise that might attract guys who had seen lots of TVs and doors at other houses, but probably hadn't smelled fresh herb-grilled chicken in any of them—not in the summer, anyway. I was never sure if that segment of the pledge class actually meant to slight me or just cared so little about food that they assumed no one would be interested in talking to the source of it, like the way you wouldn't go out of your way to talk to the utility meter reader.

But if he wasn't changed, I was, realizing that any one of those guys could have been the one we lost and that I had a certain responsibility to tread carefully. "You're going to have to tell me what I can do to help you," my husband had offered in the days after the accident. Having attended the ceremonies and seen firsthand, I guess he understood for the first time that those guys who could be so maddening and wearing on me, whom I sometimes spoke irritatingly of in the hours after work, were like my kids. We were walking in Lincoln Park exactly one week after the fall when a squirrel spotted us headed his way on the path. And rather than scurry away, he had run right up to our feet and propped himself up to get a good look at us, cocking his head, comfortable enough that you almost felt like petting him. It was like something out of an animated movie and my husband, a scientist and a rationalist—not one given to supernatural speculation—

wondered if in some way it was Kevin, returning to say hello. And of course you want to believe things like that, even when you don't believe things like that.

The accident and the effect it had on everyone in the House made me realize how self-absorbed I'd been and how I'd completely missed all the good and happy moments of that year. I realized that if I was going to stay, I needed to shift my focus, and that some things were absolutely never going to change. The plugs were going to be left out of the sinks. They were going to put one single water bottle through the dishwasher no matter how many times I pointed out it was faster to wash it by hand. Garbage would not be taken out until it was falling on the floor, and I was never going to have my own bathroom. There were going to be guys I was close to and a few for whom I was like the electrician or the cable guy. I could leave, or I could learn to laugh about it.

7

Misfit

There were two kinds of children who went to kindergarten—
those who lined up beside the door before school, as they were
supposed to, and those who ran around the playground and
scrambled to get into line when they saw Miss Binney
approaching. Ramona ran around the playground.
—*RAMONA THE PEST*, BEVERLY CLEARY

I'd only been cooking professionally for a few years before I started at the Alpha Sig House, but food had
touched my whole life. Like most everyone from south Louisiana, my family talked about dinner plans while we were
eating lunch and we wouldn't think of vacationing in places
where food wasn't important, finding it a dreary thought to
spend all day doing anything without gathering for a great
meal at the end of it. But it wasn't all about consuming; it was
about connecting. I wasn't an easy person to get to know and
I was often in trouble or out of favor in some way. But from

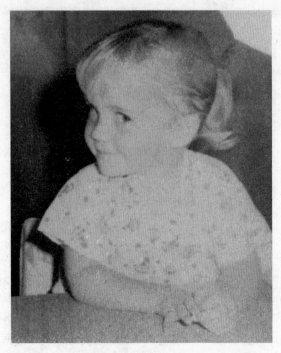

The author at age two.

an early age I knew food, and when I was a little older I could cook and that made up for a lot of other failings. I'd spent my whole life not quite fitting in with any group and there was nothing about it to indicate I would find my comfortable place in a fraternity.

I was born in New Orleans, a fact I often cite defensively to explain that I didn't need to go to culinary school or work in Michelin-starred restaurants to know what I'm talking about where good food is concerned. I was there in the second grade, the last year before my father was transferred to London, sitting in class bored out of my mind when I complained of a stomachache severe enough to require a phone call to my dad. These days I don't think you get to dictate the terms of your incarceration like that, but I was adamant that I was out of there. I was reading *Ramona the Pest* at the time, published four years after I was born, and to this day I see aspects of the central character in myself: the misunderstood rebel seeking approval, but unable to control her desire to be "the baddest witch in the whole world." My dad, on sight of me in the principal's office, knew exactly what I required. We sat by the levee overlooking the Mississippi eating a messy roast beef po'boy in happy silence, gravy and fresh tomato juices and mayonnaise running together. At the time, I only thought of my joy that someone I adored had not been mad at all, had not marched me home to bed, but instead had just understood what I needed. Looking back with adult eyes, I think he must have been happy, too, for the excuse to escape his own workplace prison.

Many years before I heard the terms "local" and "organic" and "scratch cooking," I was sitting at my grandparents' rural Louisiana tables eating freshly shelled butter beans and sweet corn from their gardens and homemade rolls and jam cake that didn't come out of a cardboard box. In one of my earliest food memories, I am standing in my maternal grandparents' garden—I could not have been more than five or six—pulling a ripe tomato off the vine in the hot Louisiana sun and diving right in for an early education on the difference between farm and factory. Sometimes, left to make my own choices, I would eat a frozen potpie or a Mexican TV dinner and the snotty liquid in the pie and metallic tang in the enchilada sauce was sort of interesting to me. I ate my share of Funyuns and chili dogs at the community pool concession stand and pink bubblegum was my favorite flavor at Baskin-Robbins. At home, weird sixties salads frequently appeared, things like canned pear halves with a dollop of Miracle Whip and shredded cheese and chopped pecans, or sometimes banana slices in place of the pear. But mostly those early years were filled with real, unpretentious meals of vegetable beef soup and stuffed pork chops and hot biscuits with cream gravy.

My father had grown up dirt poor in Turkey Creek, Louisiana, and while he escaped that rural poverty to become successful in business, his parents remained there all their lives. Yet meals at their home were always abundant. Dozens of platters of meats and vegetables and salads covered every inch of the table not occupied by dinner plates and always there were the Parker House Rolls that my grandmother made from scratch, lavishly spreading the raw dough with a thick layer of butter and folding them and letting them puff up before baking. None of my grandparents remembered the Depression as a time of particular suffering because they had always lived this way, with food of their own growing and making.

We lived a typical suburban life in Gretna on the West Bank of New Orleans, but when we visited my maternal grandparents' property in north Louisiana, we were very much in the country, where fishing and hunting wild duck and deer provided our meals. As a girl, I wasn't allowed to join the men and my older brother in the shooting, but when the dead ducks were piled on a table outside, I would help with removing the birdshot and cleaning them the same way I helped with picking the corn and shelling field peas. Having lived in times of scarcity, my elders had developed a taste for squirrel, sometimes the only meat available. I hated the cartoonish sight of them floating in a stew and loathed their slightly sweet smell and taste. But I got the connection between hunger and making use of the land and understood that if this was your only protein, you might convince yourself that the thing on your plate wasn't a dead ringer for a small rat.

My father was a civil engineer in New Orleans, my mother a high school teacher, and because my dad would leave for work later, it was his job to get my brothers and me ready for school. He would arrange my long brown hair in elaborate ponytails that some of the girls on the school bus would make fun of and pull until they conformed to the boring horsetails stuck to their own heads. It is the first memory I have of being bullied, of being someone just on the other side of the margin. But I never asked my dad to just do it "like normal," because I liked that he thought I was special and was even then not particularly interested in what the haters thought.

At the time, there were actual cooks in the schools who were not just reheating "beef" patties and frozen corn, but were making hot meals from scratch—some more desirable than others. The grits were stone cold by the time you sat your tray down and would slide off in one solid piece into the garbage can, and the red beans and rice were bland and not at all like the ones at Mother's on Poydras Street in the city, where my parents would take us some weekends. But the meatballs and the fried chicken and macaroni and cheese were all fresh and the cafeteria smelled like home on those days, not like the ammonia mixed with body odor I would smell years later when I'd visit my own kids' schools. The local paper printed the school menu weekly and my father and I would study it, circling the days that I preferred to bring a sandwich in my Jetsons lunch box with a real thermos that actually kept the milk ice-cold in the days before we sheltered kids from every conceivable threat.

And then suddenly my father accepted a job transfer and I was plucked out of the suburban New Orleans of the seventies and transplanted to London, where English was the spoken language but I could not understand a single word out of the mouths of the cabdrivers and bus conductors. And irritatingly, they did not seem to comprehend me either. Milk was delivered to the door by a milkman, of all things, and had cream floating on top. And the candy bars were all different (and better) and the sandwiches were horrible and the mustard blew your head off. We didn't shop at Winn-Dixie anymore. We bought food from the High Street where there were different shops for vegetables and meat and fish run by people called greengrocers and butchers and fishmongers, who knew everything about their one special thing. Two years after we had acclimated to life in a foreign country, the very first McDonald's opened in England and we made the seven-and-a-half-mile drive to Woolwich for a taste of home. And it was the last time we ate there, having been weaned from fast food long enough to realize that it wasn't really very good, not really any better than the ghastly native Wimpy burgers.

I gained almost all of my precollege education at the private American School in London, an institution primarily serving the kids of executives from US corporations working abroad, usually just for a couple of years. I was there for an unusually long time, save for one year in Scotland, rarely forming deep, and—because of the circumstances—never long-lasting friendships. It was a fantastically rich learning environment, where only experienced and exceptional teachers from all over the States came to work and where we traveled to Stratford-upon-Avon to see Shakespeare performed and where our French teacher would invite us into her home to teach us how to make *gougères* and chocolate mousse. But I did not fit in with the mostly Ivy League–bound kids from Boston, Massachusetts, and Rochester, New York, and Darien, Connecticut. Although my father had achieved great professional success by the time I reached my teens, we lived in a relatively modest apartment and I was fundamentally that kid from middle-class suburban New Orleans whose dad wasn't a VP at IBM or Xerox. We didn't summer in the Hamptons or on Cape Cod; we spent our summer school breaks back at my grandparents' house, thirty-seven miles from Shreveport, Louisiana.

After a year in London, when I had learned to substitute words like "lift" for "elevator" and "ice lolly" for "Popsicle," we moved to Edinburgh for a year while my father frequently traveled to the North Sea. My brothers attended public schools and I was enrolled at St. George's School for Girls, a private boarding institution that admitted a number of "day girls" like me, where my new friends had names like Fiona and Morag and Verity, which I thought were way cooler than Darlene. We were divided into Houses, groups of girls who competed in sports and academics, and the more senior girls were called prefects and had power over the rest of us—the closest I ever came to the sorority pledge experience. Besides netball, knitting, playing the recorder, and history lessons on Scottish heroes like Robert the Bruce, there were weekly discoveries of new foods.

Lunch was served in a grand dining hall where we sat at long wooden tables and there was an elevated head table at which the headmistress and more senior girls ate. I was a novelty, not just because of my accent and my rebellious failure to wear every element of the layered school uniform on hot days, but also because I was new to haggis and toad in the hole and jam roly-poly. The teacher I spent most of the day with was Mrs. Childs, a pretty young woman who gently teased me about my American usage of words like "sure," and "hi," but was not at all the severe disciplinarian I imagined in that setting, and was instead especially sensitive to the new girl, quietly excusing me from trying foreign flavors without making me feel like the weird kid. But I tried everything and, just as back home, there were things I craved more than others, like the warm custard and the apple crumble. And except for the mutton stew, which was gray and tasted like exactly what it was, *tired old sheep*, it was appetizing, all of it prepared in a kitchen on-site by people with skills beyond the use of a can opener.

We returned to England after that year and I entered the fifth grade and remained until I graduated, traveling extensively with my parents or on the kinds of school trips that even at the time I appreciated as extraordinarily privileged: choir trips to Madrid, history trips to Athens, and a three-week social studies excursion to China. On some of these travels, we were treated to hotel "tourist" meals that were indistinguishable from one country to the next, but on the street and in the markets and local restaurants, I learned more about the people than I ever did in the museums.

Once we were old enough to take care of ourselves for short periods, my mother would accompany my father on the business trips he took to Scotland or France, leaving us with days' worth of home-cooked meals in the freezer. Most of the kids I knew were similarly left and for some it was an opportunity to hold champagne and cocaine parties at their parents' rented London estates, which I only heard about, not being the sort of person who could reciprocate even if I'd wanted to. Instead, for me, home alone meant having a few of my similarly quirky friends over to cook them strange little meals that made us feel very grown-up, strange because I was new to the kitchen and because my parents did not leave us with a lot of cash. And because I knew how to eat, but not how to put together a menu, I would comb through Time Life cookbooks and Robert Carrier's *Great Dishes of the World*, choosing what looked good but having no idea how to time it all and paying little attention to yields. So we would eat all of the fried zucchini before I got around to grilling the pork chops. I also learned that one duck is not enough for six people.

I was a junior when one of these dinner-party guinea pigs introduced me to some fellow Canadians who'd just moved to London. Phil and John were brothers whose English-born mother was married to a Canadian military officer now on a diplomatic posting to the Canadian consulate in Grosvenor Square, directly across from the US embassy. As non-Americans from a military family, they were automatically different, nothing like the BMW-driving seventeen-year-olds at my school or the nice Polish Texan I was dating at the time, with whom it seemed I was headed for a very comfortable life in suburban Houston. With their long hair and jean jackets and badass attitude, they were wholly inappropriate and totally attractive.

I managed my way into the same Twentieth-Century American Literature class that Phil was taking, taught by everyone's favorite, Mr. Jesse, who, if we were reading *The Great Gatsby*, would arrive to class as Jay, fresh from one of his lavish parties—in a white tux and holding a glass of champagne. Then he'd be Pa Joad when we got to *The Grapes of Wrath*. We were fairly certain he was crazy, but he made the books come alive. He also immediately picked up on the flourishing chemistry between Phil and me, devilishly having us read the parts of George and Martha, the bitter warring couple in *Who's Afraid of Virginia Woolf?* and assigning the more docile Nick and Honey to a couple whose relationship perfectly mirrored their roles.

When it came time to apply to college, I didn't aspire to Yale or Brown like most of the girls I knew. I had no idea where I was going in life. Having always loved food, I thought about professional training and had heard about the Culinary Institute of America, but this was the time before the explosion of food television and chefs as household names. Smart girls from good homes didn't go to cooking school and so I applied to Northwestern and the University of Michigan, not because they were great schools, although they were and are, but because they were reasonably close to Ontario where Phil was in his first year at the Royal Military College of Canada. I didn't know what I was going to be, but I knew I was in love.

Shortly after I graduated and before returning to the States, Phil and I planned a three-day trip to Paris on a budget of just a few hundred dollars. My father was incensed at our unmarried travel plans and wouldn't speak to me for days. But on the night before we were to leave, he called me into the dining room where he had a map of Paris laid out, marked with his favorite inexpensive bistros and food shops and the location of Dehillerin, the famed kitchen store in Les Halles, and he described specific dishes we should make a point of ordering. I had been to the city several times with my mother and brothers and him, but this time would be different, and being a pragmatist, he made sure I was prepared. And he said nothing about our hotel plans as he handed me his map and his notes and restaurant business cards.

Accepted into both of the colleges I applied to, I chose U of M, probably because Ann Arbor was less than a full day's drive to Toronto. And because I wanted to choose a major that offered some prospect of employment at the end of four years, I chose speech therapy, despite having little aptitude for science and no interest in being a therapist of any sort. But I soon found that I enjoyed classes like art history most, despite that tough patch of the Renaissance period struggling to stay awake in a dark theater looking at endless slides of Mary and the saints. And so I changed my major to English, a subject I had competency with, even though I had to read articles about "What to Do with a Degree in English" to convince myself that it wasn't a stupid choice—and come to grips with the fact that the existence of so many such articles was probably a bad sign.

There was a large Greek community on campus, but the idea of trying to prove my cuteness or coolness or even just lack of weirdness to a bunch of girls held little appeal to someone who had always felt painfully unwelcome in the popular cliques. I already knew I wasn't part of their team, so why put myself through the humiliation of having them explain that to me? Many years later, one of my Alpha Sig guys would ask what advice I could give to a college graduate and I told him the two principles I'd learned from my parents that had helped me through those first years on my own and for all the years after. From my mother: "Live beneath your means." And from my father: "Think for yourself." And it was that latter advice that in time made me completely comfortable going my own way.

Ann Arbor is now known as a great food town, but either

because it wasn't so at that time or because I didn't have the income to experience it, I became obsessed with vicariously enjoying what I'd grown up with and was suddenly without. In a used bookstore, I found old copies of *Gourmet* magazine and bought several stacks of them, reading them like trashy novels and taking notes on recipes to try at some future date when I had more equipment than an electric kettle that boiled water and heated canned soup. I created menus for all kinds of imagined future events, though I'm fairly certain that when I actually married and had babies and lots of friends to entertain, I tossed them all for something more affordable and manageable than the kinds of servant-requiring meals suggested circa 1953. But it didn't matter that I was neither creating nor consuming the ballottine of chicken breast stuffed with shrimp mousse on a mustard and cognac cream sauce. I just liked to think about it.

U of M was a magnificent school, both architecturally and academically, with a lush campus and classes taught by the same people authoring the textbooks, but I was deeply unhappy there. It was more than just missing Phil, who I held very tightly and sadly when we ended our rare visits. It was that I had chosen a school where I had no family or cultural ties, no friends from high school to share in that first uncertain year, and no club to belong to, being neither an athlete nor, I felt, particularly gifted at anything that anyone might find attractive. At one point, I stood in the shower severely depressed and sobbed, glad that even if someone did see me there, I could hide the tears in the water streaming down my face. Just thinking that way made me feel like the ultimate loser, so that in later years when I heard about a college freshman writing herself out of whatever story had been hers with a jump or a gun, I would remember being right there.

But it was the first of what became several points in time when I would decide that no one else was responsible for my happiness and that if I hated my life, I should change it. So I applied to Queen's University in Kingston, Ontario, the same town where Phil was at Her Majesty's pleasure, gaining an education in return for years of military service postgraduation. And while I had little cultural connection and no family there either, I did have the one high school friend who really mattered, so all the potential stress of a new environment was mitigated by the comfort of sharing it with someone I thought of as stronger and more stable.

I moved into a one-bedroom student apartment and while he was supposed to live in military college housing, Phil essentially moved in with me to the most stripped-down place we were ever to call home. We had nothing and for a while slept and ate on the floor until we scored a cheap bed and a vinyl-covered table with four matching yellow-and-brown chairs for a little over $30 from a secondhand store. And when I saw the slightly larger married quarters of a "mature" fellow student, I marveled at the microwave and stereo and lamps, all luxuries to someone who was balancing scrap wood on two piles of books and calling it a coffee table. But unlike Phil's friends, we had our own place with a kitchen so we could have people over for dinner, even if we couldn't offer the kind of food that warranted the title "dinner party." I knew that Tex-Mex might be cheap, but it screamed festive! And there was no one who didn't like pasta with homemade tomato-cream sauce, which you could call vodka sauce even if it had no liquor. No one would really notice. But of course, when you could afford it, you would throw it in there and claim it made all the difference.

For our everyday meals, I learned that if you adopted the

right attitude and were generous with seasoning, you could view beans on toast topped with shredded cheese as a fine dinner. And I learned that it was not really cheap to go coupon crazy because the coupons were never for fresh food and you could make a ground beef and noodle dish for less than the cost of the boxed version with better results. Although I was not above making King Ranch Chicken with prepared cream of mushroom soup, I was revolted by the same product dumped over canned green beans and crowned Holiday Favorite, arguing rather irrationally that because I was seasoning the soup and because you couldn't readily identify it in the King Ranch, it was okay. It was like the way my grandmother, for all of her scratch biscuits and homemade beef stews, would not bat an eye at serving a Cool Whip, marshmallow, and canned fruit cocktail frozen salad at Thanksgiving. But she wouldn't think of plopping the same petroleum "cream" on her huckleberry cobbler. She topped it instead with electric-cranked vanilla ice cream from one of those machines where sometimes the salt in the ice got into the frozen dessert, making it even more delicious—long before salinating desserts was trendy. And so years later when I became more conscious of everything I cooked and ate, I would remind myself that Velveeta had once or twice crossed my lips without killing me and I would remember to be less sanctimonious, lest someone find a box of Oreos in my current pantry and call me a liar.

To the obvious disapproval of my professors and classmates, I spent my final year of college with a wedding ring and an ever-growing belly, taking my last final exam two weeks before giving birth to our first son. It didn't help that at twenty-one I looked about sixteen and when my doctor confirmed my condition, the very next words out of his mouth were "I don't do terminations." Like the high school I had attended, Queen's was then, as now, a place where privileged and bright people went to become someone, like maybe prime minister. The other women in US-Canada Relations and Literary Criticism and Theory were not only having a ripping time at the bars that I was obviously not patronizing, but they also had immediate goals that didn't include husbands and babies. So I wasn't just an American alien to them; I was an *alien*.

My husband's college experience was similarly odd, since he had chosen his school for practical reasons rather than any great desire to conform to military college orders and instructions and was at least once on the verge of expulsion for having a normal life with me outside of the fortress walls of Point Frederick. Finding *VENEZ-ME VOIR, ATQP* (COME SEE ME, ASAP) on a sign posted to his door was an unwelcome invitation from superiors that he expected to see every time he returned to his living quarters. He was a top student academically, which was the only thing that saved him, and there were others like him who became our close friends, most of them leaving the service years later as he had, as much for a more self-directed life as for higher salaries.

Our son Sean was born on the Tuesday before Phil's Saturday graduation and while we were thrilled with our healthy baby, who lifted his head to check it all out within hours of arrival, I cried constantly for days. I felt guilty about it, unaware of what was happening, because unlike the older moms I would know subsequently, I hadn't read all the books to prepare me for feeling like a crampy, deflated beach ball with warring thoughts of both adoration and rejection. And I guess neither my mom nor Phil's, both of whom were also practically child mothers, had wanted to warn me about feeling possessed by demonic voices. When I held his little swaddled body in my hospital bed, I had this obsessive thought that he was going to grow up and hate me, that the little pink heart-shaped face and adoring blue eyes shouldn't fool me. But of course I realize now that I was twenty-one years old with this enormous responsibility on top of just the regular hormonal shock.

In some ways, though, it was great to be young parents. Because we had no money, we couldn't go out anyway. So Sean was not just our entertainment; he was also adopted by the other twentysomething military couples we knew. We didn't have the financial resources to trick out a nursery, so while he did without the latest in baby interior design, he had our almost full-time attention, undistracted by important business meetings and travel. And for the first weeks of his life, he didn't have a home anyway. Instead he had a car seat, as we packed up our one-bedroom student apartment and made the cross-country drive to Moose Jaw, Saskatchewan, Phil's first military posting, the prairie town where he was to begin pilot training.

Our first stop was in Hearst, Ontario, a remote northern town where 85 percent of the population was French speaking. Checked into our nondescript motel room, we sat at the adjacent restaurant, where we lasted less than the time it took our server to approach us as Sean wailed, landing every eye in the place upon us. And so I sat on the bed in our nonstarred motel room holding my infant despondently as Phil set out to find a take-away dinner. He returned an hour later, not with the cold burgers and fries I expected, but with a bottle of wine and a box, which when opened revealed trout in a cream sauce topped with toasted almonds, a rice pilaf, and crisp haricots verts. I cried as I looked up at my resourceful husband who knew that the best way to turn this whole night around was to skip the easier options and find a real restaurant willing to package up one of the most memorable meals of my life—which we ate with plastic forks on a threadbare bedspread while Sean slept, oblivious, nearby.

I had grown up in an increasingly comfortable household, but during those early postcollege years, my husband and I lived on his $20,000 starting salary. And while he worked a job whose danger far exceeded its compensation, I stayed home with Sean in a house divided into four apartments that backed onto railroad tracks and wheat silos. In the twenties, Moose Jaw had been a boomtown of bootlegging, gambling, and prostitution—a reputed retreat for Al Capone. But by 1985, a thirty-two-foot, ten-ton fiberglass Mac the Moose was the only tourist attraction and the city was best known as the home of a prominent politician who was on trial for bludgeoning his wife to death. We had exactly two special date options: The first was a brightly lit restaurant with plastic placemats that we ate at only once after our server apologized that our dinner was delayed because our steaks were thawing in the microwave. The second was a dark, velvet-draped hotel dining room where a waiter who appeared to be plucked from 1960 flambéed every course like he had just invented the technique. The nearest major city was Regina. With a population of less than 170,000, Regina was reputed at the time to be the murder capital of Canada. And Edmonton, a relative metropolis at four times the size, was nine hours away. So it was hard for me to tell if my slight postpartum depression was about the hormones or about the desolation of living in a place where the temperature for a great part of the year could reach minus twenty degrees and you worried your tiny baby would freeze solid on the trip from the front door to the car. Or possibly it had something to do with the oppressively hot summer, when swarms of grasshoppers made it hard to walk and covered your car in crushed bodies and blood.

But we were not alone; some of my husband's classmates from the Royal Military College had received the same posting and several of them were married, though not yet parents like us. With little money and few entertainment options, we took turns hosting dinner parties in a town where the produce manager at the local grocery store described limes as an exotic ingredient that wouldn't sell if he stocked them. But somehow without limes or goat cheese or fresh herbs or duck breast, we managed to pull off approximations of the recipes in *The Silver Palate* and Martha Stewart's *Entertaining*, and no matter how expensive or elaborate future dinner parties were in bigger cities, they never quite matched the fun of substituting seven out of ten ingredients.

I loved that I could say I had lived in Moose Jaw, trumping anyone's claim to having had a hard start in married life, but when my husband failed pilot training and became a combat systems engineer in the navy, we were ecstatic to trade the dismal prairie town for Victoria, British Columbia, proving that failure is often nothing more than golden opportunity. And for the next four years, we lived there and then in Nova Scotia on the east coast, where we had a second baby, bought a cute little house on cozy Cranberry Crescent, settled into the stable life of a military officer's family—and realized that at twenty-six we had stopped living. So we did exactly the opposite of what prudent people do and listed a home we had owned less than ten months, quit our jobs, and moved into an apartment in Halifax while we waited for the US Immigration and Naturalization Service to grant my husband and sons visas to start a new life with less predictability and more possibility.

My parents had returned from London to settle in Lafayette, Louisiana, a couple of years earlier and we moved into their house so that my husband could attend graduate school on a fellowship of $1,000 a month. It was August when we arrived and less than two months later, my father attended a business gathering in New Orleans with my mother and never returned. When a family friend came to the door to tell me that my dad had collapsed in a restaurant, I heard the words, but they made no sense to me put together like that. She had to say it several different ways before I understood that I would never see him again, this man who had most shaped my ideas about food from the day twenty years earlier when we sat on the levee eating our po'boys. We had been there just before he made his own leap to a different life in a new country with small children, a leap I had just made. I thought about how this man who had never slept more than four hours a night had often joked, "I can sleep when I'm dead," and how he detested the expression "killing time," and how he was always taking bold steps and savoring a life that just suddenly stopped at fifty-four years.

Shortly after the loss, Phil abandoned the PhD path he was on and took his masters in computer engineering and a research position at LSU in Baton Rouge. It was a temporary measure until we figured out our next leap in life, which turned out to be a seven-year stint in Fort Collins, Colorado, after Phil accepted a job offer from Hewlett-Packard. It was a busy and rewarding time for Phil and for the first five years, Sean and Simon were young enough that I had a role to play, although I never identified with art mom and PTA mom and all the other women who treated copying and cutting and chaperoning as an actual job. I knew that all of that volunteering was necessary and appreciated, but it wasn't the same as having something completely separate to talk about at the dinner table, something other than whether Bradley was a burgeoning psychopath and whether the kids could tell if being in the Elephant Group was better or worse than being in the Rabbit Group. As the years passed, I saw Phil grow professionally and the kids grow into their own separate lives, and there were times when I felt irrelevant.

When HP was seeking engineers willing to transfer to Texas, Sean and Simon were in the tenth and eighth grades, hardly an ideal time for a move. Predictably, they resented us for uprooting them, while we saw the change in environment as healthy, because we had moved around all our lives. In the boys' new high school, I found that art mom and PTA mom had become band mom, sinking so much of her own identity into her child that I wondered if she was going to follow her graduating senior to college. And maybe I was a terrible mother, but I was determined to not memorize my kids' class schedules and to not be that mom still making her kids' lunches, complete with a note and a smiley face. If I'd had a career, I think I might have done those things ironically, but as it was, I feared the slippery slope toward empty-nest insanity.

My mother, who'd had a career teaching high school in New Orleans, gave that up when my father accepted the transfer to London. And while she never became one of those all-day Bloody Mary–drinking spouses that typified the American Wives' Club, she did fall, somewhat uncomfortably I always felt, into the role of full-time wife and mother. I remembered how much lighter and happier she'd seemed when I was a small child, how she would sing to us in the car as she drove us home from Kiddy Koop, and how the singing stopped when we moved. Years later she quietly confided to me, not with any bitterness but more a frustration at herself, that she regretted "all those hours and hours playing bridge when I could have worked." When she told me this, she was into a second career as a tax specialist, a job she started in her fifties. And I understood by then that it wasn't the wife and mommy part that she resented; it was the wasted time when my brothers and my dad and I were not even there.

So when I took the job cooking for college guys, I was looking for a thing of my own. I wanted a challenging project and while I could have taken other kitchen jobs, none gave me the freedom of this one. It was mine to turn into whatever I could imagine, "like your own restaurant," Bob had said at my interview. But it gave me something else I couldn't have found just anywhere: people who needed me, some who loved me, and a place to belong.

Black Bottom Pie

In college, I kept a notebook that I still have in which I hand-wrote recipes in my kitchenless dorm room, hungry for a lot more than food. Some of the recipes were from magazines and some were passed down from family members. My dad was not a cake lover and would request this fantastically rich and wonderful pie for his birthday.

Make pie several hours or the day before serving to allow time for the filling to set. Just before serving, spread whipped cream over pie and sprinkle with almonds.

1 cup fine gingersnap crumbs
3 T. melted butter
2 cups milk
1 cup sugar
2 T. cornstarch
1/4 tsp. salt
3 eggs, separated
2 1-oz. squares unsweetened chocolate
1 tsp. vanilla
1/4 cup cold water
1 envelope gelatin
2 T. rum or 1/2 tsp. rum extract
3/4 cup toasted slivered blanched almonds
1/8 tsp. cream of tartar
1/2 pt. (8 oz.) whipping cream

Blend gingersnap crumbs with melted butter and press firmly into 9-inch pie pan. Bake at 350 degrees 8–10 minutes. Cool. Scald milk in top of double boiler over hot water.

Blend ½ cup sugar, cornstarch, and salt and stir into the hot milk. Cook and stir until thickened. Beat egg yolks lightly. Stir slowly into hot mixture. Cook and stir until thickened. Melt chocolate over hot water. Stir 1¼ cups of the custard and the vanilla into the chocolate and beat till smooth. Turn into gingersnap crust. Chill. Soften gelatin in cold water and dissolve in remaining hot custard. Cool until mixture begins to jell. Stir in rum and ½ cup of almonds. Beat egg whites with cream of tartar until stiff. Gradually beat in remaining ½ cup of sugar. Whip ½ cup cream until stiff. Fold meringue and cream into thickened custard. Heap over chocolate layer. Chill until firm. At serving time whip remaining ½ cup of cream. Spread over pie and sprinkle with almonds.

Parker House Rolls

These were always on the dinner table at my paternal grandparents' home. The smell of sugar, butter, and yeast as these baked was almost better than actually eating them.

2 cups whole milk
½ cup (8 oz.) butter
½ cup sugar
1 pkg. yeast
½ tsp. salt
6 cups flour, divided
extra butter for brushing on dough, softened to room temperature

Heat the milk, butter, and sugar in a medium heavy saucepan until the butter and sugar melt. Remove from heat and let sit until barely warm. Dissolve yeast with salt in a little water and add to milk mixture. Add 3 cups of the flour, stir, cover with a damp cloth, and let rise to double. Dump onto floured board and add about 3 additional cups flour. Return to bowl. Cover with damp cloth and place in refrigerator.

When ready to use, knead the dough, pull off pieces of dough, and roll each into an oval shape. Brush with softened butter, fold in half, and press lightly. Place on buttered baking sheet, almost touching. Cover loosely and let rise about 1 hour. Bake at 400 degrees 15–18 minutes or until lightly browned.

Perspective

It was only after Kevin's death that I saw all the positive things about the year that preceded it and realized that a lot of my unhappiness was of my own making; the pledge class had not been uniformly difficult and much of the stress came from demands I put on myself. Another job wasn't going to offer me anything I couldn't create in my current one and it was probably not going to give me the one thing that I most treasured, besides the guys, of course: total control over the menu and dictatorship in the kitchen. I pulled out the group picture taken the year before and circled all the faces of guys who *didn't* drain every drop of energy out of me, and when I saw that it was most of them, I knew I'd focused on the wrong people and that not only could I do this job, but I wanted to. I thought that if I could just see things a little differently, things would be different.

So I went back to work for a third year, which was also a historical election year in which the "old dude" and the "black dude" were candidates and where the normally harmoniously heterogeneous House was divided. Despite having been raised in a Baptist Republican family, I was pretty obviously not a far righter, but I did my best to keep my opinions to myself. What was more immediate on the minds of the guys was that it was clear that the country was not just in a little bad spot, but that the Western world's financial foundation was on the brink of collapse. It was a terrible time to be anywhere near college graduation, especially if you, like 90 percent of the guys in the House at that time, were an undergraduate business major. So I could count on being cheered up about my own circumstances just by having one of them sit in the kitchen and tell me about his day. Not that you want to rejoice in someone else's misfortune, but there was nothing like hearing about being unemployable, $50,000 in debt, and involuntarily celibate with an as-yet-unwritten thirty-page paper on credit default swaps due in five hours to put your own crappy day in perspective.

Eventually things settled into an ordinary depressing recession, and everyone just got used to accepting that they were not going to get that job as sports editor for the *Seattle Times* with a B average in English from the UW, but rather that they'd be lucky to sell ties at Macy's right out of school. Everyone accepted a new normal of drastically lowered expectations, but for a while it seemed like the country was going straight to hell.

So it was a challenging time to focus on the funnier parts of my job, which I decided I needed to do if I were going to remain. In an effort to take control of my happiness, I did practical things like padlocking the dining buffet tables together so that they wouldn't continually disappear for a new life in basement beer-pong service. And I put a note on the freezer that it was a *freezer* for *my* use, not a cooler for Jell-O shots or a quick chill-down spot for their beverages. But duct tape, chains, and hundred-pound weights could only prevent certain behaviors and notes just invited trouble. Freshman Ryan learned this when he posted a sign on the front door announcing: WHOEVER FUCKED WITH MY SHIT I AM LITERALLY GOING TO BEAT THE FUCKING SHIT OUT OF YOU. FUCK YOU!!!

Besides wanting to suggest a thesaurus, I had another piece of advice for Ryan and felt particularly qualified. Feeling similar sentiments myself every single working day for the past two years, I sympathized. But I predicted correctly that this was only the beginning of his woes, and shortly afterward his pledge brother Trevor added his own response anonymously, HA, HA, RIGHT! telling everyone that girls from Alpha Alpha had been both the cause of Ryan's original rage and the taunting note writers.

I felt for Ryan, but I knew from experience that he was just asking for it. I would still lose it at times and post notes like: DO NOT PUT JUST ONE GODDAMN CUP THROUGH THE DISHWASHER AT A TIME, or EATING THE CRAB BISQUE LEFT OUT OF THE FRIDGE OVERNIGHT WILL MAKE YOU HATE YOUR LIFE. But I would remove them minutes later, realizing the futility and not wanting to be further demoralized by the inevitable snarky rejoinders. I had to constantly tell myself that no matter how right I was about everything, I wasn't paying the bills or spending the day in the bathroom swearing off seafood forever.

THE FIRST TEST OF my newly adopted more easygoing attitude came early in the fall when someone called 911 to report gas fumes and then headed off to class, leaving me to talk to the three firemen standing in the dining hall, wanting to question the caller. Freshman Johnny had announced their presence to me, oblivious in the kitchen while they searched the House. "The fire department is here and they are *pissed*." After finding nothing, they demanded to know who had made the false report, and I don't know what possessed me, but all I could think, after repeatedly telling them that I had no idea who'd called, was that I was like the Little Old Lady Who Lived in a Shoe. "Y'know," I said as they stared at me, obviously having not been read to enough as babies, "I have so many children I don't know what to do. I'll give them some broth without any bread and whip them all soundly and send them to bed." For what felt like a very long time, they stared at me and said nothing, seeming to forget why they were there, and I made a mental note to try something similar on the health inspector. Maybe "Little Miss Muffet" or "Three Blind Mice."

What I hadn't counted on was that as I began to see the funny side of the guys, they returned the effort by pointing out every mock-worthy moment in *my* behavior. Newman and Dan, now confidently enrolled in their third year in the House just as I was, were particularly fond of illuminating my gross inconsistencies. "Weren't you just on a rant about that sort of thing?" Newman inquired as he watched me pouring packaged ranch dressing mix into sour cream the day after decrying a certain orange powdered cheese-like substance. And Dan became the fake food inspector, scouring the kitchen and fridges daily for hypocrisy alerts. "What do I see here?" he'd ask, knowing very well that what he saw was prepared clam chowder from Ivar's, where he bussed tables. I felt bad enough about the ranch mix, especially when I read the package and saw that it was clearly made by Clorox—the same foodcentric company that made bleach and cat litter—and I stopped cold. I kept the packets for a while anyway before finally taking this guilt-inducing crutch to the food bank, about which I felt even guiltier because I was passing it off to people who already suffered from a lack of adequate nutrition.

Newman and Dan were vocal conservatives, viewing me inaccurately as a raving liberal, so much of their goading had nothing to do with food and everything to do with scoring points in a game I wasn't even interested in playing. Still, while you got used to your own kids dismissing you as stupid until they got old enough to realize what a genius you'd always been, you felt professionally attacked when your customers questioned your consistency and credibility. And in that way Newman and Dan more than anyone else pushed me into a more fervent stance against processed food, because, while I had no qualms about using them as comedic fodder in my observations, I refused to be made fun of.

And it wasn't just processed food they were all over my ass about; it was everything I professed. They waited to pounce on every inconsistency, the way your kids catch you talking on a cell phone one goddamn time while driving and never let you forget it. "I was just wondering," Badley inquired innocently, "why you were serving *that* on Yom Kippur," as I pulled braised pork shoulder from the oven. Badley wasn't Jewish, but he had heard my sermons on diversity and cultural sensitivity and knew that sophomore Jesse *did* keep kosher, a fact the pork victim kept to himself for a whole year because he was too polite to be a problem for me. And just when I learned of it and was doing my best to leave bacon out of the twice-baked potatoes and collard greens, there I was dishing out pig on the holiest day of the Jewish calendar, as if I meant to. And from then on it became a joke between us, Jesse frequently inquiring which of the side dishes I was hiding the pork in today.

Just as the guys who'd started the same year I did had become secure enough in my love for them to turn me into an object of ridicule, guys who had recently graduated began this year to return specifically to see me. Meaker, who'd been a senior and the house manager when I started, had moved out after my first year, but he continued to come by to sell the guys on opening accounts with U.S. Bank, where he worked postgraduation, and also to talk food with me. "I started keeping duck fat," he told me, having heard that I felt happier seeing a fridge well stocked with solid golden duck fat than I would feel seeing my closet stocked with a dozen new pairs of shoes. But he had no idea what to do with it and had just thought that if I said it was a good thing to have on hand, then it was. And he kept looking at it, waiting for it to make him happy, too. "There's nothing better than potatoes cooked in duck fat," I suggested as he watched me pull red wine–braised brisket out of the oven, but he didn't seem to be listening and was instead peering at the beef as I sank a fork into it. It was a shock to the guys to move out and discover that not only were there no pledges washing their dishes, but that freshly cooked meals didn't appear at 11:00 and 5:00 every day.

Meaker had always taken an interest in the menu when he'd lived in the House, suggesting classic dishes as if I'd never heard of them. "There's this sort of beef stew you put in a pan and spread mashed potatoes over it and then you get it brown and crusty on top," he'd say. "Shepherd's pie," I would reply, and he'd seem disappointed that it had a name and that *I* knew what it was. He assured me that he was cooking proper meals now that he was on his own, but he seemed awfully taken with the brisket I was inspecting for doneness. "That looks sort of good," he critiqued before claiming he had a plan for dinner already and then told me he actually had used some of that duck fat. "I made grilled sandwiches for some friends, with pancetta and pear and pepper jack cheese and I fried it in the fat." When I smiled in astonishment, he added apologetically, "Well, pepper jack was the only cheese I had." He was just about to leave when he turned and asked me if I happened to keep one of those to-go boxes in the kitchen and off he went home with red wine–braised brisket for dinner.

When Newman, whom I'd always found unfairly critical of the lovable and harmless Meaker ever since he was a pledge three years earlier, heard about this, he told me that if I kept feeding the graduates, they'd keep coming around like stray cats. I guess this was supposed to make me stop, but it had the opposite effect. I loved that they were drawn back and was sad when their visits tapered off, hoping that it meant they were cooking for themselves or that they had interesting new lives. There was nothing more pathetic than the one or two who continued to come to frat parties years after graduation, when even some of the current residents had stopped. Newman was a freshman when Meaker lived in the House, but for the new pledges, these alumni were strangers and it was odd to be the one person besides Bob who had memories of people beyond three years.

Among the twenty pledges that year was Carlos, the first in his family to attend college and an unlikely frat boy, having grown up in a blue-collar household that seemed to have left him with a powerful appreciation for every material thing he had. I first noticed this when he brought a package into the kitchen that had just arrived from his mother and opened it, thrilled like a kid on Christmas morning to find it full of clean new T-shirts. He had not intended to join a fraternity but had received a letter from Alpha Sigs encouraging him to consider a life that he was sure would be hostile to "a poor Mexican kid from Eastern Washington." He was about to toss the letter when he looked at the House website and saw Eliab, the current president, staring him in the face.

Eliab was one of several African Americans in the House and had been a sophomore when I started my job, a little guy with a huge wit whom I always remembered as one of the first to jump into kitchen tasks unasked when he could see that I was about to lose it in my first few weeks. He'd become president by this, my third year, the year the House was accused of racism for having hung rival Washington State's mascot from the front porch. They showed up to a disciplinary hearing to point out the obvious fact that this was the only House on campus with a president who wasn't white. "A black dude as president of a frat?" Carlos later exclaimed to me when I asked him why *this* House, why he had not even considered another.

We bonded over our mutual hatred of late plates, a system I managed to quietly kill that year, in which guys who couldn't be bothered to show up for dinner would sign their name to a whiteboard requesting that a pledge assemble a meal in a to-go box, write their name on it, and place it in the fridge. I had my own view of this, describing it as entombing a perfectly good meal in an environmentally friendly coffin to be incinerated later in the microwave. But besides the professional sense of being dissed, having worked all day to provide a meal at its optimum state only to have someone treat it like a frozen dinner, I hated the way it disrupted the whole point of communal living, communal dining being the most important of all the rituals. And the freshmen not only hated that they had to prepare these care packages, but also that they were constantly berated for not doing them well, Newman going so far as to draft a formal letter of complaint:

Carlos and his pledge bro Adam make the absolute worst late plates I have seen in my 2 years at the Fraternity (unless of course the recipient is Sergio who today received 3 times the amount of chicken in his late plate as the rest of us did). The portions I have received in my late plates would be considered meager for a person of small stature and a light build (Zach for example). Being an average sized male, I simply cannot survive on just one 6 oz. serving of chicken and 4 oz. of bow-tie pasta. For this reason I have found it necessary to prey upon the late plates of certain people living in the House who tend to receive relatively generous amounts of food on a regular basis (Sergio). As a political science major, one of my primary interests is legislation and policy and the incentives necessary to enforce them. I play my part every day to create incentives to show up in time for dinner and soon those people who have until now enjoyed generous late plates, will begin to see their plates devoured by Newman before they get a chance to partake. Because of this risk, there is now an increased incentive to eat the meal at 5:00 pm because there is a chance that if they don't, they may open the fridge to find no dinner at all.

P.S. Should Adam or Carlos read this, be very aware that people are watching you.
Sincerely,
Newman
Executive Member at Large and Late Plate Enthusiast

When the late plate sign-up whiteboard, which I had mystifyingly purchased from Office Depot with my own money, fell off the wall, I saw no good reason to spend additional funds replacing it. There were numerous inquiries about its demise and plans for its return and yet not one person thought to buy another one. Even the industrious guys who could be counted on to pick up a Christmas tree or a barbecue pit or a new flat-screen TV for the House seemed incapable of solving the missing-board problem. For a while, guys would scratch their name on a piece of scrap paper or a coffee filter, and the list would inevitably fall to the ground to be stepped on or find its way into the trash. But no one bothered to just *go out and buy another whiteboard*. And magically that was the end of the late plate.

You could stop an undesirable behavior by making it hard, but weirdly you couldn't encourage them to, say, wipe last night's spaghetti sauce off the lunch table by putting the bleach bucket and a rag right next to it. Similarly, they would complain that the cereal dispensers were empty when there were spare bags in the cupboard right below, claiming that they couldn't find them. But I was pretty sure that if I took to storing the whiskey and rum I used for chocolate walnut pie and tiramisu in those very same cupboards, I'd be making a lot more trips to the liquor store.

By November, my efforts at attitude adjustment were challenged by the reality that while I had changed, the guys had not. I had been around long enough to know that my mornings would sometimes be complicated by parties and rituals that had occurred the night before, but this usually meant that I would simply have to navigate my way through an apparent crime scene in the basement lit by swirling purple lights, watching my step for broken glass and body fluids. Except for this morning-after exposure, I was detached from the party side of fraternity life. Of all the misconceptions about my job, the most common was that it must be an environment more like Bourbon Street at Mardi Gras than a professional kitchen. But in fact, except for Greek Week, the parties were a once-a-week affair, held long after I'd gone home for the night. Still, I heard enough about them to know that there were several different sorts of "frat party," all generating various degrees of morning-after regret:

The Cocktail

This was the first type of party I heard about on my second day on the job when a senior asked me if I was going to "make food for our Cocktail." I imagined martinis and canapés and told him that I didn't see how I could fit that into my workload. But he set me straight with descriptions of the former cook dropping off trays of Costco shrimp and vegetable platters to accompany the "grape" wine, a disappointment to the girls who preferred "hard A" but a step up from the Keystone Light.

The Grab a Date

No matter how many times one of the guys explained this to me, I never understood what it was or how it differed from the Cocktail, but I assumed it was as desperate as it sounded, given the number of times one of them would ask *me* to be the grabbed date and then seem genuinely crushed when I laughed it off.

Get Tanked

Straight to the point, but actually this was one of a number of theme parties, complete with camouflage curtains and military props transforming the House into something that looked like a cross between a video game and a paintball setting. I couldn't imagine girls attending this particular themed event, but there were others that seemed only slightly more appealing if for no other reason than the coveted "hard A" was on offer.

The Halloween Cruise

An alcohol-free tour around Lake Washington or Lake Union on one of the city's short cruise lines, this was an argument if ever there was one for abandoning the farce and lowering the drinking age. The guys and their dates would take a chartered bus from the House to the boat, or at least that was the plan, because a good number of them would be forbidden entry onto the bus, having downed a fifth of vodka before the first bite of frozen egg rolls. With all of the preparty excitement and energy to pull together coordinating costumes followed by crushing letdown, this form of party scored second highest on the effort-to-enjoyment ratio.

Formal

Number one on the effort-to-enjoyment ratio, Formal was always held in Vancouver or Victoria across the border, where the drinking age was a more realistic nineteen. With everyone able to sip wine with the overcooked chicken plated dinners, there was no need for clandestine empty-stomach intoxication, but the distance and the expense guaranteed a bad time for most. What to the guys was a stressful and costly ordeal was to the girls a free trip across the border, prompting one of my guys to defend himself to me with the memorable, "I'm not using her for sex; she's using me for Canada!"

I KNEW ABOUT ALL of this by now in a way that neither appealed to me nor really affected me. But this particular Friday morning in November I couldn't remain detached when I found access to my freezer completely denied by furniture stacked up inexplicably against the door to the basement, where some form of party had unfolded the night before. I had by now reduced the number of things that would set me off to one overarching theme: anything that kept me from the tools to do my job. "I don't give a crap about the broken glass on the stairs or the whole gallons of milk left out on the tables," I would lie. "I just need to be able to cook." And because there was now just *one* thing on my nonnegotiable list, it was all the more infuriating when they crossed that line.

So on this morning I stormed up the stairs to the kitchen, where I confronted sophomore Steven, a quiet Asian American who had seemed indifferent to my cooking and was not a regular visitor to the kitchen. But there he just happened to be, the unfortunate first person on my warpath, and I confronted him accusatorily with, "What the hell?" I was so angry that I had not actually wanted an explanation, but Steven responded nonresponsively with "I don't know; I hardly live here anymore." I suddenly felt a kinship with this person whom I had never warmed to before. He was one of those guys I could never understand who went all the way through the months-long obstacle course of initiation and then decided to move out, remaining a member but without enjoying any of the benefits of all that bonding.

But that morning I got it. "I can see why," I said as I unlocked the kitchen and asked him to text Jesse that if I couldn't get to my freezer in the next ten minutes there'd be no lunch. I expected him to go away and leave me alone with my rage, which, like my husband, most of the guys knew was the best course of action. But instead he followed me and planted himself on the kitchen stool with a bowl of cereal in his hands. He sat there and chatted for a solid hour, at one point asking me why I had so disliked him the previous year when he'd been a pledge—one of those pledges from the horrible year. "I'm lazy," he had declared when I pointed out the half-assed job he'd done on dish duty. He'd said it not in a self-critical, apologetic sort of way. It was more the way you'd say, "I'm a paraplegic," expecting to be cut some slack on removing the grease and food scraps out of the sink, as if laziness put you in a protected class.

"I'm on my feet all day, ten hours a day," I explained. "So I have no patience for indolence." He seemed to process this and I wondered if it would have made a difference the previous year if I'd just been more clear, less hotheaded. I had a tendency to make quick judgments and sometimes just wrote guys out of my life script, which is exactly what I had done with Mr. I'm Lazy. It is exactly what I had done with that whole pledge class, until that hour when he forced me to talk to him as I busied myself with the work that didn't require a trip to the freezer. And there was such a thaw that I forgot how the morning had started and was receptive to his request for chicken soup "because half the house is sick right now."

I had not planned on this and so delivering on the promise required a special trip to the grocery store and the purchase of chickens "*at my own expense,*" I pointed out, leaving out the fact that I could have requested reimbursement if it had really been the hardship I wanted him to think it was. I would sometimes have to explicitly state my wonderfulness, because after a while they'd become complacent and just expect impromptu gifts of chicken soup, while cooks at other houses got a round of applause just for showing up to work. A few days later, I found a thank-you card in my kitchen from Steven with the annotation that he had purchased the card. At his own expense.

Just as the guys would invariably ask for refills on deli meats at the moment I'd plunged my hands into raw chicken butchering, or would ask for peanut butter the second I had returned from the remote food storage area, requests for things like chicken soup would always come the minute after the food ordering cut off. Badley was one of those who I was certain had been the kid who asked his mom for five dozen cupcakes the night before a school bake sale. It was a few days before the Christmas party, one of the busiest weeks in my work year, when he approached me with a request. "I was just wondering," he began in that ominous way I'd learned to translate as "I'm about to ask you for a major readjustment in your carefully planned day." "I was just wondering if I could make scrambled eggs," he asked me, which really meant, "Can I squeeze in here and get in your way and make a mess?" "No," I told him flatly as I handed him one of the boiled eggs

I was trying to clear out of the fridge. I explained pointedly that I was expecting an unusually large delivery because of Saturday's Christmas party and that I would be very, very busy squeezing prep for that into my regular meal duties. But he didn't seem to get what I was saying. "Well, I was also wondering," he plowed on, "if you could make something sweet and delicious for my German class."

Newman, Dan, and Zach were in the same class and sometime before they'd told me about an attempt by their instructor to engage them in conversational German. "What time do you start cooking dinner?" she had prompted. And Zach had replied that he didn't cook anything; he had a chef. Perhaps sensing an attempt to avoid more extensive vocabulary, she had posed the same question to Newman, who gave the same answer, with the same blank expression, followed by Dan. By the time she got to Badley, she was on the verge of losing it and met his answer with a response in German that they were all either very uncooperative or very spoiled. So while I was tempted to hand Badley some space-hogging oranges as my "sweet and delicious" contribution to the class party, I was also aware that expectations were higher than a bag of fruit. Pride and a stubborn determination to provide something handcrafted usually won over practical considerations like having no ingredients and no time, and so the three went happily armed with chocolate-covered toffee that I made that night at home.

In the two previous years, the Christmas party, held on a Saturday, had been for me an unwelcome addition to an already full workweek, but in that third year some of the guys made it less burdensome by reversing the usual trend of suddenly being absent at just the moment I needed a hand. Junior

Zach, who'd been one of Kevin's four spring pledge brothers, was especially helpful, offering to run errands for no apparent personal gain and without the usual passive-aggressive attitude I often got from guys who helped in a way that left no doubt that this was a major imposition on their "me" time. So when he and Jesse popped their heads into the kitchen on Friday to ask if I needed anything from Costco, I assumed they were purchasing supplies for the party. They were, but not in the way I had thought, as I realized when I asked them what they already had on their list. There was an awkward pause and an exchange of uncomfortable expressions between them before Jesse managed to find the word. "Protection," he said. And for just a second, I imagined a gun purchase, before realizing that they were uncomfortable using the word "condom," despite having no qualms at all about leaving the used items themselves in my path to the pantry.

It was not like Jesse to be coy or to edit himself. He was someone who couldn't just say great, when you asked him how he was. Rather he would say that his day had begun "in the best possible way . . . if you know what I mean." He greeted brokers who came by pedaling processed food with, "Our chef says you're a crap pusher." So it was odd to see him suddenly shifting uncomfortably. At times like that I found it best for everyone if I just acted like we were talking about broccoli and asked if they would mind picking up some party napkins in addition to the . . . broccoli. "Oh that will be gay," Zach burst out, uncharacteristically resistant. "Two guys buying protection and party napkins." They returned from their trip without my request, but with the unmistakably heterosexual fine bottle of wine, condoms, and a lavishly illustrated book from *Vogue*. And not because I was overly interested in the guys' sex lives, but because my mind was free to wander while I carried on the tedious task of tying up fifteen tenderloins for roasting, I wondered what sort of bulk packaging the "protection" came in and whether it was something they shared, like the first aid kit and cases of hand soap—or whether Jesse was having a *lot* of great mornings.

On the Saturday of the party, Dan and Newman kept me company in the kitchen, running platters of food out so I could avoid the dreaded small talk with parents, with whom I acted like the nice lady who cooked for their sons. Some of the parents had heard that the real me was often cranky, swore a lot, had a tendency to email wine-enhanced ranting missives to my food supplier, and didn't always see the golden side of their sons. I had feared a backlash from overprotective parents expecting a more nurturing and sunny-natured cook, but the most benignly critical comment came that night from a mom who thanked me for making the chicken soup for her sick son, a reassuring sign to her that I wasn't really, as she put it cheerfully, "as horrible as a parent might think." But still, I felt pressure to be someone quite different in their presence, a feeling shared by a few of the guys.

Winter break coincided with a city-crippling storm the press dubbed Snowpocalypse, during which unsalted roads and insufficient street-clearing equipment kept residents confined to their homes for more than a week. Steeply inclined Queen Anne Avenue was closed to vehicles and became a snowboarding and sledding hill and the Seattle Police Department declared that it would respond on foot to any calls from the city's several hills, including Upper Queen Anne, where we lived in the very uppermost part. Uncollected garbage started to spill out onto the icy streets and cars and buses stood abandoned for days so that it began to look like a scene from a nuclear disaster movie. With everyone in the city deprived of their usual routine, unable to Christmas shop or walk a block without falling on their asses, a heavy sense of unease hung in the air and it was hard to tell the truly crazy people from the ordinary citizens weary of the daily struggle.

Because I was the sort of person who kept things like cheese biscuit–wrapped dates and sausage rolls and beef chuck roast in the freezer, and canned tomatoes and treats like brandied peaches and sour cherry jam in the pantry, my husband and I were better off than most. But I knew that the guys who had elected to live in the House over break were faring worse trying to stretch out the half a pan of chicken potpie from the last supper and making their twentieth quesadilla with the cheese and tortillas I'd left in their fridge. And so I pulled a bourbon chocolate cake that I'd intended as our Christmas dessert out of the freezer and implored my husband to drive me down the treacherous and lawless streets to the Alpha Sig House, where I left my gift with a note that the cake was saturated in quality bourbon. I left the note not only to emphasize the point that I had just risked my life for them, but also to let them know that I'd sacrificed twenty dollars' worth of Maker's Mark to their cause. I heard later that Jesse had found it too alcoholic—a memorable first.

The city became livable again just as I returned for winter quarter, the dullest of the three working terms, falling during the dreariest period in Seattle: January through March. It had none of the exciting newness of fall quarter nor the brightness and casual atmosphere of spring. And the stews and root vegetables of the previous months seemed as worn as the clogs I would buy each September. Having failed on the Jewish dietary front on Yom Kippur, I attempted to redeem myself with the Catholics on Ash Wednesday.

Over the years, the number of practicing Catholics fluctuated, but that year there were at least a dozen, some of whom made it clear to me that they would not eat meat on Fridays during Lent. I'd heard of forgoing desserts and tobacco during these weeks, but until I worked in a fraternity, I'd never heard of giving up Facebook, texting, and my favorite, "buying weed." They weren't talking about *using* mind you, just *paying* for it, which placed the abstainer at the unpredictable mercy of his less pious friends. So seriously did some guys take the dietary restriction that I decided to make Ash Wednesday meat-free for everyone, both at lunch and dinner. I reasoned that it wouldn't kill anyone to have a good old animal cleanse and prepared a lunch of pasta with a roasted eggplant marinara and a beans, greens, and grains dinner that went over about as well as if I had served roasted koala bear. "Some people weren't happy," one of the sophomores told me. He went on to say that in protest "someone" had taken cold leftover steaks from the fridge and had stood there chewing away like a Neanderthal in front of the Catholics.

The day before Ash Wednesday, I had been so stricken by some ailment that I could barely stand up and had forced myself to get through until I collapsed on the TV room couch, where Badley found me immobile. "If you can't come in tomorrow," he had said, "it's okay. We'll manage. I don't know how, but . . ." And it was obvious as his voice trailed off that he was not so much concerned that I might die right there in the next ten minutes, but rather that he was taking mental notes of what he could hoard to get him through the day without a cook. Except for a couple of weather-related absences,

I had never missed a day of work, but that following Ash Wednesday I might just as well have stayed home. It was also the last time I attempted mandatory vegetarianism. Years later, one of the guys approached me furiously waving the *Daily*, the UW student paper. "Have you seen this?" he asked, as outraged as if the campus were becoming an all-female institution. "No meat on Mondays in the UW dining halls!" And I thought back to that shunning and assured him that even though recent studies had linked meat to sudden death, "That is never happening here."

After spring break, the threat of religious holiday food failure was over and it was an easier time for another reason: The guys stopped requiring Friday dinner and instead required that I order hot dogs and hamburgers and leave them to cook the weekly rush barbecues for visiting high school seniors. And this third year a new tradition started that gave me one extra day off. I think it was Newman who introduced the idea of a pig roast on the Thursday of Greek Week and I'm sure that what they envisioned was a group chest-beat around a fire with eyeball- and brain-eating dares. I'm not saying it *wasn't* that, too, but I knew the whole thing would require of them planning, cooperation, and a predawn lighting of the coals, all things that would keep at least some of them sober and civil for a whole day until the pig reached 155 degrees long after I was gone. So I said that this was a budget-stretching treat, which was true, but I was quickly on the phone to my food sales guy Kirk in search of a pig.

We needed it to come in the day before my regular delivery so that it would have time to soak up the rub I planned to make, which meant that Kirk had to make a special trip from the warehouse, a thirty-mile journey he was clearly not relishing. A natty dresser and someone generally fastidious about his environment, he balked at the idea of transporting a whole dead animal in his own car, the creature being far too large to fit in his trunk. So after the third time he indicated it would be coming in with my truck delivery on Thursday, I stressed that it had to be Wednesday and told him to put it in the passenger seat with a pair of shades and a wig and take the HOV lane.

At the time, I didn't have a walk-in cooler and my two commercial refrigerators were already packed with food. We considered removing the shelves from the guys' refrigerator and standing the pig up inside, which might have worked except that I had been cooking in a frat house long enough to know that leaving something like that in an unlocked cooler overnight during Greek Week was just not a good idea. "We could wrap duct tape around the fridge," Badley suggested, which I knew was like putting a sign on it declaring HIGHLY DESIRABLE CONTENTS. So Newman made arrangements with Zeta Zeta Zeta's cook to leave it in her walk-in and after I rubbed it with a spice mixture and wrapped it in plastic, he and Zach hauled it away, one holding the head and the other the feet, a head-turning sight up two blocks to the better-equipped sorority house.

Despite its dramatic appearance turning on a spit, a sixty-five-pound pig does not feed a crowd, so I prepared several pans of pulled pork, baked beans, and potato salad and bowls of fresh pineapple. All day long, the guys took turns adding coals, basting, and putting out flames, all with the sense of purpose I had hoped for. The sorority guests recoiled at the sight of the spinning pig, its bronzing and cracking skin provoking exclamations of "eeew" and "gross" before the girls dove into the pans of the less visually carnal pulled flesh bathed in sweet barbecue sauce. The next morning, crows were picking at what little remained on the carcass. I heard that the pig finally came to temperature after sunset and that Devin had eaten the eyeballs and Jake had devoured the brain. They boasted about this as if hoping for shock, but I was thrilled they had wasted nothing of the animal, and instead had eaten things they would respond to with revulsion if they found them on the dinner line.

That year, the alumni-gathering Founders' Day fell the Saturday immediately following Greek Week, an unfortunate circumstance requiring the House to be immaculate at the worst possible time. Something happened to frat guys once they graduated, making them less tolerant of bongs on the landing and barf in the bathroom sinks. And while most of them had cooks they fondly remembered only because they couldn't remember the food, or very well recalled the abundance of grease and gristle, they somehow expected a fine meal for Founders' Day. I had escaped this duty the two prior years, having two sons graduating from college in successive years on the same weekend. But since I couldn't invent a third child, I grimly accepted the task of preparing dinner for 120 on a Saturday. Because I had wanted to simplify the serving process, I planned a room-temperature menu of salmon, beef tenderloin, and tomatoes stuffed with an artichoke-rice salad. It sounded wonderful on paper, but the actual task of hollowing out 120 tomatoes and filling them one by one was made even more tedious by Badley exclaiming, "Looks like a waste of time to me!" It was one of those things you watch people eat with pleasant indifference and you want to scream, "That was backbreaking work so you goddamn well better *love* it!"

I had stressed the importance of a streamlined menu because my helpers were to be a team of volunteer sorority girls, apparently selected for their charm rather than any food-handling experience. I was skeptical because the last time I'd had such assistance the girls had arrived looking like the entertainment. "We're your help!" one of them had said brightly, though I thought the only thing they were going to be helpful for dressed like that was waking up the more elderly alumni. "Tell them to dress like they're visiting granny on her deathbed," I suggested to Badley when he seemed mystified as to what sort of wardrobe tips to give girls who he thought looked fine as they were.

In subsequent years, I learned to stop cooking well before the last day of finals. No matter how I tried to establish a head count, the numbers of eaters dropped off considerably each day. I posted a calendar of the week, asking the guys to write their names on the last day they planned to eat and all of them specified Friday, but it was something they did as a sort of insurance policy against starving, even though they knew very well they would be headed home before the end of the week. So that particular Friday I looked in disgust at the guys' fridge, which was packed with enough flank steak, scalloped potatoes, spaghetti, and pork chops to feed ten houses. I was decrying the waste when Shane, a sunny-spirited Californian and our most civic-minded freshman, suggested packaging it all up in the much-maligned and now-unused late plate boxes and delivering it to the U-District food bank. "This has the potential to turn out very badly," one of them fretted, which I thought applied to just about every one of their group endeavors—except this one. And so I smiled warmly as I watched them head out the door. A couple of hours later they reported that the food bank had rejected them, explaining the hazards of accepting prepared food. So they walked a block over and handed out boxes to the hungry homeless, who seemed far less suspicious of frat boys bearing gifts.

It did not go very badly; it went in such a way that I more than forgave them for creating the problem in the first place. And I went home that summer feeling a reluctant softness toward them that had not been there a year before. In the first two years, I'd been insistent that this was my workplace and that they were my customers. But now I saw that this was their home and they were people, not employers, and you couldn't neatly separate your work from their lives. I had learned to laugh just a little bit more—at myself as much as them. But I was also restless and knew that if I was going to stay, I needed a bigger challenge than ditching the packaged ranch dressing and the Pace salsa, and I set out to spend my summer looking for it.

Salsa

I realized at some point that I always had ingredients on hand to make a salsa a thousand times better than anything commercially available. It's the number one recipe request from guys about to graduate. Organic tomatoes really do make a huge difference and in the summer if you can get vine-ripe fresh ones, use those instead.

1 28-oz. can whole organic tomatoes
1–2 cloves garlic
hot peppers of some sort (1 or 2 fresh jalapeños or a
    couple of canned chipotles in adobo)
¼ medium red onion
¼ bunch of fresh cilantro, stems included
salt
fresh lime juice

Puree ingredients from tomatoes through cilantro in a food processor and stir in salt and fresh lime juice to taste.

Pimiento Cheese

Not being from the South, where this is common at parties and gatherings, my guys were unfamiliar with it, calling it "that cheese dip" and requesting it often. No rigid rules on this except you have to use freshly grated cheese; pregrated won't give you the right texture since it's coated in I don't know what, some kind of powdery crap. The classic is just cheese, mayonnaise, and pimiento, but this is mine. The proportions are up to you; use as much cheese as you wish and then play around with the other ingredients.

Anonymous request on kitchen Magnetic Poetry board.

freshly shredded sharp cheddar cheese
diced red onion
diced pimiento peppers
diced pickled or fresh jalapeño peppers (totally
   not traditional)
smoked paprika (ditto)
mayonnaise

Mix this together vigorously. The idea is to create a chunky but spreadable paste, which you serve on crackers. This is also used as a sandwich filling in the South, although I think it should be served on something crisp or crunchy.

Rub for Pig Roast

Originally created for our annual pig roasts, but you can use this to season pork shoulder before braising in a low oven for several hours. Leave out the sugar if you use this to season pork chops, where the direct high heat will cause the sugar to burn.

1 cup Hungarian sweet paprika
$1/2$ cup smoked paprika
$1^{1}/4$ cups freshly ground black pepper
$1^{1}/4$ cups sugar
10 T. salt
$3^{1}/2$ T. dry mustard
$3^{1}/2$ T. cayenne pepper

Stir everything together and store in an airtight container.

Down and Dirty

When Ramona made a great big noisy fuss, she usually got her
way. Great big noisy fusses were often necessary.
—Ramona the Pest, Beverly Cleary

I'm not sure how it was that I stumbled across the website of Quillisascut Farm School of the Domestic Arts in
Eastern Washington. I think maybe it was when I was looking
for information about their goat cheese, which I'd heard was
a fine example of artisan food production in the state. In any
case, I had wanted to find a substantial project for that summer after my third year at the fraternity, something to inspire
me with ideas for the following year. And there it was at the
place that produced the cheese I was investigating: an intensive five-day course on a farm. The guys, knowing my preference for cleanliness and orderliness, not to mention my
fondness for active city life, thought this was a hilarious idea,

but I had been moving in the direction of getting close to my food for a long time.

If this was new to some of the guys, it was not at all a surprise to my food suppliers: Rod and his salesmen and the delivery drivers who talked to me often about what I was buying and what I *wanted* to buy. One morning Tommy, my food delivery driver, explained that he was late because he'd just spent the past half hour having breakfast at another fraternity house while the chef peppered him with questions about me. "What's she like?" he'd pried, apparently having heard rumors that I was out of the norm. "Well," Tommy had replied after some thought as to how to put it, "she's petite, not much over five feet. And she is feisty and scrappy." He had called me hardcore on another occasion when he'd heard me falling down the stairs with a case of tomatoes in my arms and I'd rejected his offers to help as I dusted myself off and assured him that I was just fine. Tommy had been a restaurant cook at one time and would often comment on the items in my delivery, praising all the fresh produce and occasionally ripping into me when there was something he didn't approve of. The other fraternity chef had asked to see my invoice to verify the rumors that I was buying outlandish things like raw meat and organic salad greens. Tommy said he couldn't show him that. "But I can't stop you if you want to come look in the truck." And the chef had done just that.

Years after his humble visit to plead for my continued business, Rod, now director of sales at the company supplying most of our food, sent me a birthday email of a woman cocking her head and exclaiming, "I'm comfortable enough around you now to let you see little snippets of the horrible fucking monster I really am." The woman was obviously supposed to be me and I could laugh about it because I wasn't just now getting around to showing him what a monster I could be; I'd been doing it for years and proudly recognized this about myself. With my incessant demands for something better than the garbage indifferently dropped off at most other "institutions," I was a tough customer.

Admittedly my antics went far beyond demanding the best food for my guys. I would do things like email Rod and his sales reps a photograph of the heads of lettuce I was paying for by the piece next to a 1.5-ounce bag of chips with the subject line, "Lilliputian Lettuces," or a picture of a "pound" of butter on a scale showing 15.3 oz. I'd complain that my box of seventy-count potatoes was one short. And then one day, when I noticed that the five-pound box of lemons seemed awfully light, I remarked about it to Tommy before putting it on the scale. "Not even 3.5 pounds. Try again," I wrote on the box before handing it back to Tommy to return to the warehouse.

The next day I received a forwarded email from accounting with the terse message that customers were forbidden to write on boxes of product, that they would credit her this time, but that she was on notice. And I emailed a response that if I couldn't write on the next half-empty delivery that would be the *last* fucking box of lemons I bought from them. Before I worked in a frat house I wasn't like that at all. I was too unsure of myself and too fearful of consequences to be anything but passively troublesome. But working here had emboldened me and I'd become someone who couldn't wait for a screwup so I could find some way to totally piss off an uptight manager. And I think that really I was doing all of this not only because it was funny to me to irritate people happy with the status quo, but also because I really wanted to be heard, because while the guys and I reveled in these little moments of trivial fun-poking, there was also a serious and sincere side to my complaints.

The more I read the more I thought about polluted shrimp farms and confined cattle and things I was pretty sure were not making for the most delicious food. And when I would see TV commercials for preboiled bags of potatoes that featured a woman too stupid to stick a potato in a pot of water, or kids incapable of making a peanut butter sandwich after school who were somehow able to microwave a box of frozen pizza-like things, it didn't seem like progress at all. So while I wore on Rod's nerves with my emails about huge "fingerling" potatoes with the message "they're not called 'armlings' for a reason," there were things about the food industry that genuinely troubled me.

When I started cooking for the Alpha Sig House, my goal was simple: to provide the kind of scratch home cooking I'd grown up eating and fed my own kids. But I learned over time that it was actually really hard to find simple food. I was an easier customer in the days before I began to ask questions about where our products were coming from, what was in them, and why. In an early attempt to pacify me, Rod sent a meat rep to answer my questions, and by the time I was done, it was clear that he and I were not going to be swapping recipes. He couldn't tell me where any of the meat was from or whether the ground beef came from one or ten countries, except to say that none of it was from farms in Washington State.

And he visibly chafed at being questioned by a little woman who was implying that his meat was not good enough for her. The attempt having failed, Rod gave me a motivational book on positive thinking. I did read it and I did find its tips on coping with my own whining and complaining customers useful. But I didn't think it applied to me at all; I was right when I whined and complained. I thought we'd have a better food system if we all adopted a little more bad attitude. And I didn't think what I was asking for was crazy at all, because my grandmother, who no one would describe as either flaky or elitist, had described her own past experience with sourcing meat in this way:

> We raised maybe ten or twelve hogs to kill every year. You had to wait until somebody butchered and when they did, you bought from them or you swapped. And then you'd butcher and they'd help eat yours.
> We didn't have a market. I don't even think they sold fresh meat in our town.

In the summer before my fourth year at the fraternity, I arrived at Quillisascut Farm for an intensive introduction to rural self-sufficiency. I wanted to find a place where people ate without a trip to Safeway or 7-Eleven, and actually killed their dinner instead. I'd read plenty about understanding where food comes from, but I was seeking a more direct experience; I wanted to get down and dirty. The particular course I had chosen was limited to culinary professionals, a title I had a hard time bestowing on myself. I also worried that I would feel a little like the pledges, thrown in with strangers in dormitory sleeping and showering arrangements, with the notable difference that I fretted there'd be no liquor for four whole days (an unfounded concern as it turned out), which would make it even harder to get over the social awkwardness of being the one who is not like the others.

It's a three-hundred-mile drive from Seattle to Rice, Washington, and while Rice is only eighty miles from Spokane, its remoteness from the nearest interstate makes even that a several-hour journey. So by the time I reached the farm, the physical isolation matched the awkwardness of making small talk with the other "culinary professionals" who'd arrived before me. There was a restaurant critic, a pastry-chef-turned-teacher, a group from high-end food management company Bon Appétit, and several Seattle and Spokane chefs who already sourced from local farmers, having the money and time that I lacked. They didn't work alone in a house of eighty guys with a $48 per person weekly budget, so they did not have to rely on the big food distributors and let me know bluntly that buying from Sysco and US Foods put me in a lesser league. But I disagreed with this and argued that significant change was only going to come when the companies who supplied schools and hospitals and frat houses started listening to big noisy fusses from people like me.

Clearly they thought I was an idiot. And I felt like that slightly chubby fifth grader being picked last for PE volleyball teams when we split into the groups that took turns planning and preparing meals. And those meals could not include chocolate or lemons or anything we couldn't source from either Quillisascut or from one of the neighboring farms and orchards—or from the wilderness. It was afternoon when we arrived and we ate plates of cheeses from the milk of the farm goats and a dinner of:

GRILLED CHICKEN

GRILLED RADICCHIO AND FENNEL

HERBED WHITE BEANS AND LAVASH

CHÈVRE AND HUCKLEBERRY PUDDING CAKE

Every element was either raised or grown or made on the farm. And as we sat around a long rectangular table with only ourselves as entertainment, it reminded me of those hours-long family gatherings I'd experienced as a child, except that here we were all self-consciously *having a freshly cooked meal together*, whereas when I was a kid it was just supper.

When the farm rooster sounded the alarm the next morning, I rushed to the edge of the property to watch the sunrise and then headed back to the house for the optional witnessing of the goat slaughter—optional for us, not the goat. I had grown up around hunters and fishermen and the connection between the animals around us and the thing on the plate was so obvious then that I didn't think about it. But something in the intervening years had made me see this as a major event, and not one I was looking forward to. Rick, the co-owner of the farm, had decided that our sacrificed goat was going to be one of the males who'd been especially difficult and aggressive in recent days, a little detail that perversely made my mind wander to my job, until he said that the male in question had put up no resistance and instead seemed resigned to his fate. He slit the throat out of our presence, having experienced unpleasant kill viewings in the past, and he told us that while it was never an easy thing to do it made you intensely aware that you were taking a life and made you feel responsible for using it well. So we encountered the animal moments after death, lying still in the grass, and we watched as Rick tied him up by his feet so that the goat hung spread-eagled ready to be skinned and gutted. When Rick invited us to help in the skinning, to run our hands between the hide and the flesh, it felt less like an invitation than a moral obligation. And when you did slip your hand in, the flesh was so warm that you were acutely aware he'd been alive, running around, being an aggressive doomed little bastard less than an hour ago. And you knew you were not going to waste one part of him.

We removed his heart, which we saved for that night's meal, and we cut him into roasts and chops and made sausage from the pieces too irregular for anything else, giving the scraps to the dogs. We used the bones for stock. And we wrapped the caul fat, the fat surrounding the organs, around meat patties to fry for breakfast. None of the goat went into the garbage and only one person in the group, the same person who seemed to have missed her flight to Canyon Ranch spa and ended up here by mistake, had the gall after all of that to declare, "I'm not eating goat!"

That night we ate a meal of:

Goat Heart Crostini

Lamb Loin with Tomato Jam

Green and Wax Beans

Farro Tabbouleh with Peppermint
and Spearmint

Homemade Bread

I didn't touch a computer all four days, but I received several texts, one from graduate Perry still seeking guidance from me, this time on a roasted chicken dinner for his girlfriend, and three from soon-to-be-senior Zach: one reminding me that it was his twenty-first birthday, so he could have his first drink ever, one asking me what I planned to cook for his special day (nothing, as I had no plans to drive back to Seattle for his benefit), and a third proclaiming "that's messed up!" to my response that I was turning off my phone for the remainder of my retreat.

The farm staff had prepared our first meal, but each of our four-member groups was responsible for the rest. We were to plan, execute, serve, and describe our menu and because this was a course for culinary professionals, there was a competitive atmosphere. My team members were a corporate cook who seemed to be there on obligatory assignment, an energetic and talented female chef from a well-known Seattle restaurant, and a Spokane chef-owner determined to assert his alpha maleness over this poor hand he'd been dealt that included the obviously useless frat cook. I was happy to let the two restaurant chefs bicker over how long to keep the goat stew in the wood-fired oven and whether to roast or braise the fennel, but I drew the line at accepting the help they wanted to offer preparing the deviled duck eggs, the one menu item they had reluctantly delegated. "I think I've got it," I assured Ms. Real Chef when she stepped in to instruct me on the use of the food processor. I presented my creamy duck eggs to the group feeling like a five-year-old making toast for Mothers' Day.

Having exhausted the possibilities of one farm animal, we turned to chickens on our third day, holding them upside down and chopping their heads off with an axe on a tree stump, dunking them in boiling water to loosen their feathers, and plucking and gutting them in the fresh air, with the eerie occasional crowing sound when someone touched the vocal cords in a particular way. And when we were done, we lined them up in hotel pans and their small, slightly yellow bodies looked nothing like the frozen white slabs in plastic bags at Costco. We made apricot jam, four types of bread, several kinds of cheese using milk from the farm goats, and we picked huckleberries in the wild and swam in the nearby lake. When our competitive dinners were over, we gathered on the porch in the August heat and drank wine and talked for hours, there being nothing else to do.

It was during one of those wine-fueled nights that I got the irresistible urge to sneak out to a local business rumored to be owned by a family supporting "white nationalism." I'd been bothered on my early morning runs to see his TURN RIGHT HERE sign at the side of the road and in the sober light of dawn had smiled at the thought of swiping it and putting it up on the southbound side of the Aurora Bridge in Seattle to mark the way to Queen Anne. We joked about this as we drank our wine on the porch, about how we could each take turns hanging it somewhere and sending pictures to the owner, and the more we talked the more serious the compulsion to break from the group. I walked some considerable distance in the pitch blackness, and felt slightly panicked as I got close enough that I could see the lights inside the owner's house. But I wasn't about to back out now and pulled my prize from the ground, surprised by how heavy it was and alarmed that I was now going to have to haul it back to the farm—a woman alone on a country road running with a suspicious object in her arms. Most of the other culinary professionals found it hilariously fitting that the frat cook had actually gone through with the prank they'd only joked about, but the staff at Quillisascut were not so amused and I returned it the next morning, feeling like the very bad girl that I was.

On my way back to Seattle from the farm, I bought a case of apricots from Cliffside Orchard with a plan to turn some of them into an apricot custard tart as a belated birthday gift to Zach and to dry, pickle, and can the rest. I had other ambitious plans for work, like making sausage and butchering whole animals, and after hearing me list my goals, my husband asked if I'd considered making my own air. On my list of summer experiments was homemade crème fraîche, which I'd wanted for years at the House to make a three-ingredient potato gratin: just potatoes, Gruyère, and crème fraîche. And when I told the cashier at the grocery store that I needed non-ultra-pasteurized cream to make this luxury item for a fraternity, there was a hush over the store as customers in line leaned in to hear me describe the simple process:

*You just heat two cups of non-ultra-pasteurized cream
with two tablespoons of buttermilk to eighty-five
degrees, remove from the heat, pour it into a jar, and
let it sit for twenty-four hours at room temperature
until it thickens and then refrigerate it.*

But from the looks on their faces, I couldn't tell if it was the recipe they wanted or confirmation that they'd heard me say this was for a *fraternity*.

I did make the tart and delivered it to the House, a place I made a point of avoiding from June through August after that year. During the summer, the kitchen was unlocked and used by the guys, none of whom seemed to know that you have to empty the grease trap and replace the dishwasher chemicals. You could sort of forgive that, but from appearances, no one ever wiped the counters, mopped, or seemed to understand that if you leave broken eggs on the tiles for more than an hour, they become your new floor. I knew that they would return it all to something approaching the state I'd left it in before I came back to work, but there was something disheartening about seeing spaghetti and barbecue sauce stuck to the walls and an inch of crusty food on the grill that they kept adding to over time, like the way a tree adds rings in successive years. I dropped off my still-warm and glistening tart amid all that mess and wondered, not for the first time, if I was deluded.

I had gone to Quillisascut Farm with the specific purpose of getting in literal touch with my food. And I had hoped that the real chefs on the same course could help me find afford-able sources for beef and pork and chicken that didn't come from massive industrial factories where the animals were packed together like a box of crayons. I didn't find those answers and it was to be a few more years before I started to feel less crazy for asking, but I did find something else: triggered childhood memories of catching, gutting, and grilling fish at Chicot State Park in Louisiana, picking and hulling field peas on my grandparents' patio in the hot summer sun, and seeing row upon row of fig preserves lined up on the counter after a day of pulling the abundance of fruit off the trees before it all rotted. They were memories that made me realize that what I was after wasn't new at all. It was just lost.

We raised almost everything we ate in the garden. Your grandpa loved to see things planted and see them come up. I remember one time I made some kind of dish. We had company and your grandpa liked to brag about his garden and he said, "I raised and cooked everything you see on that plate." And I just sat there and didn't say a word.
—GENEVIEVE THOMAS EVANS, MY GRANDMOTHER

Deviled Eggs

You don't have to be a professional chef to make these, but I'm surprised by how hard it is to find a properly hard-cooked egg (minus the gross green ring) in either home kitchens or your average restaurant.

6 eggs
2 T. mayonnaise
¼ tsp. dry mustard
salt and pepper to taste
**other stuff of your choosing (fresh herbs, smoked
    salmon, capers, etc.)**

Cover eggs with cold water and bring to a boil. Remove from heat, cover, and let sit for 10 minutes. Rinse thoroughly in cold water to stop the cooking (overcooking is what causes the gag-inducing green stuff). Peel. Slice in half. Scoop out the yolks and combine with other ingredients. Spoon into the hollowed-out whites, or pipe in the filling using a pastry bag and decorative tip for more visual appeal.

10

Team Players

Don't let the fact that you can't do everything make you do nothing.

—Lora Lea Misterly, co-owner of Quillisascut Farm

On my last day at Quillisascut Farm, we sat around the kitchen table sharing what we had learned and how we intended to put that into action in our jobs and our lives. When attention turned to me, I stumbled because I didn't have the answers. We weren't going to raise goats at the Alpha Sig House, even though I thought it was a brilliant answer to both a local cheese supply and cleaning up the trash. And when I'd previously asked Bob for a strip of yard for a vegetable garden, he had agreed to an unused narrow section on the south side of the House that was helpfully free of traffic and uselessly free of sun. All the goat milking and cheese making and getting my hands dirty and bloody was deeply enriching to my soul, but I was on my way back to reality and resistance, or so I thought, unaware of the supportive new team that would enter the picture that year.

Newman had left for Germany for a quarter of study abroad—studying beer and women from what I gathered. He defended this by assuring me that the beer was "of excellent quality and cheaper than water," without saying anything about the women. And he sent reports on the farmers' markets, but admitted that he was mostly living on bratwurst. Zach, Dan, and Jesse moved into a "live out," a sort of halfway house where groups of seniors shared rent close enough to the Alpha Sig House that those who wished could continue to eat and party at the fraternity by paying a "social bill." There were two groups of guys who chose to forgo the meal plan: those who liked to cook, which made me happy in a sad way but glad that I had instilled in them a desire to create instead of just consume even if it meant I saw less of them, and those who believed they could eat more cheaply on their own, which was true if they were willing to lower their standards and radically increase their sodium intake. The seniors moved out to make room for an ever-expanding pledge class, but Badley, the newly elected president, remained in the House.

In the summer before his presidency, he asked me to prepare a letter introducing myself to the new pledges and their parents. Each year, the House leadership prepared a packet for the incoming freshmen, but it had never included a note from me. It was supposed to be a friendly orientation, but I believed in laying ground rules and submitted a letter for Badley's approval, which read in part:

> As to my reputation for being mean, it is categorically not true. I simply have two very firm requirements:

1. Sanitation in the kitchen and dining area. This should be self-explanatory, but let's be perfectly explicit: if you make a mess, clean it up; if you take something out of the fridge, return it before it develops enough bacteria to kill someone; clear your plates and throw away your trash. We receive frequent Health Department inspections from a very sarcastic, nitpicking inspector. Even more sarcastic and nitpicking than me. Don't embarrass me.

2. Respect for my work area and the tools of my job. I come into work at 7:00 a.m. and I need a clean and stocked kitchen right from the start. So please don't block my parking spot, put a six-pack in the freezer, break into my kitchen or pantries, or unplug cooling equipment, leaving food to spoil. Not that anyone's ever done any of that.

I knew that Badley considered this a joke when he sent the email, "Well, hey, so could you send me your real letter." I had thought about sending it as a PDF so he couldn't mess with my words, but it proved unnecessary and Bob approved it, sending it out to freshmen whom I could tell the first time I saw them were split into two categories: those who hated me before day one and those who didn't need the lecture. I'd written it in the naive belief that they behaved the way they did because they lacked guidelines and that a few helpful tips would magically improve my work environment. And I learned from this that there was little to be gained from providing an instruction manual on the location of my buttons and how best to push them.

Since so many of the guys I'd been close to had moved out, I took a special interest in trying to learn the names of the incoming freshmen within the first month, taking pictures of each of them. In the past I had immediately learned the names of those I liked most and least, with the majority languishing in obscurity until they did something to make themselves memorable, for good or ill, which a few never did. They were all in white T-shirts with their names and home cities written on them in permanent marker the first day of Work Week, most looking shy and awkward or nauseous, but the pledge whose T-shirt read RICHARD from the farming community SEDRO-WOOLLEY stood smiling broadly with two thumbs up. Scanning through the photos at home, I stopped at his picture, number ten of twenty, and wondered what the happy approval was for, because unlike me, who would pose like that in obvious derision if I were hauled out of bed at dawn to scrub floors, Richard looked like he'd won the lottery.

There were others pictured whom I would come to know well, but all of them blended together as I looked at them that night, an unusually homogeneous, conservative, and clean-cut lineup. And then there was Riley, hair buzzed off and looking completely different than when he'd arrived the previous weekend to meet his new brothers. He'd shown up a few days earlier looking like he'd wandered in straight from the slopes. He was tall and skinny, and with his long hair and goatee, board shorts and breezy attitude, he seemed a complete misfit in that group. And while many in that crowd recoiled at the sight of him, he immediately won everyone over with his antics and impersonations and his ridiculous laugh. While everyone else was nervously doing as they were told and trying to stay beneath the radar until initiation, Riley was completely out there; even the picture of him that day with his head shaved seemed more like mockery than conformity.

. . . .

I PRINTED OUT THUMBNAILS of all twenty-two pledges, writing their names underneath their pictures. My husband suggested that I cut them out and create magnets so that I could stick the ones who were on my shit list on their fridge, a kind of passive-aggressive way to improve my work environment. And while Riley would predictably appear on that list with regularity, Richard never did.

The guys called him Little Dick to distinguish him from the other Richard in the pledge class, whom they dubbed Big Dick, despite the latter's being not especially big and not a dick either. For a long time I used the nickname, too, until I decided that not only was it embarrassing, but it also didn't fit the person who, while small in stature, immediately asserted himself as a leader. He was from the Skagit Valley north of Seattle where both of his parents worked, his father as the county prosecutor. And he had a younger brother about whom he seemed especially protective. It wasn't until years later that I learned from his own admission that he didn't love everyone; he was just very skilled at getting along with everyone. And because of that, there was no one who didn't love *him*.

Pledge Blair, on the other hand, was someone I could count on to tell me exactly what he thought, not just of me but of everyone else in the House, and every*thing* else, too. And because he immediately glommed on to me in much the way Badley had, he earned the moniker Care Blair, as in *Darlene's* Care Bear in human form with the conveniently rhyming name. He'd come to UW from southern Washington where he'd grown up with brothers and parents who were divorced, though apparently not acrimoniously, and with whom he seemed to have a positive relationship.

Like Richard, he worked a fair number of hours to pay for some of his expenses and did so without drawing attention to it; unlike a lot of guys their age, they took out the trash when no one was looking and obviously had not been raised by parents who gave them five bucks to brush their teeth or get to school on time. And as with all the pledges, he had dishwashing duties, but he carried his chore out so well and with such an absence of drama that I forever after insisted he teach others little tips like placing bowls and pots *upside down* in the dishwasher. "That's just common sense!" I railed to him one day when another pledge had followed this transgression by placing the bag of garbage I'd left for him to take to the Dumpsters outside into *another* garbage can in the House.

Along with the shake-up in House leadership and the influx of these new recruits who made each fall very different from the last, I lost my food sales guy Kirk, or rather I fired him in a friendly sort of way that we would argue about later. But in any case, after three years, it felt a lot like a breakup and made me uncomfortably sad. I'd grown really fond of him, despite frequent conflict over late deliveries and missing or incorrect items; he'd put up with a lot, suffering my immature and inexperienced rants over the phone when things didn't go my way. "Have you ever even heard of a Chinese salmon?" I had screamed at him after my delivery driver had already correctly assessed my displeasure at the sourcing label on the box with the rhetorical, "I guess you won't be wanting the fish?"

Kirk had always been so calm, taking ten seconds before replying, but he had also seemed to treat me as slightly less important than I thought I was, placing a higher value on more lucrative customers like casinos and hotels. It was a rational triage of priorities, but the day I waited hours for him to bring me the replacement fish that was sitting in his car while he prospected one of those more profitable customers was the day that I got on the phone to Rod to plead for a change in personnel. When Kirk met with me the next day, I broke the news of his firing as he sat on my kitchen stool eating a sandwich I'd made him. "I understand," he told me without emotion, and he continued to visit, over time revising history to argue that John had "stolen my favorite customer."

It was John, a brand-new hire of Rod's, who replaced Kirk. And far from stealing the account, he was assigned the task of dealing with a customer known to be challenging. "He doesn't have a clue," Rod had told me when I asked him if he'd briefed his new guy about me. I was referring to how demanding and sharp-tongued I could be, which I viewed as passion and others called a pain in the ass. And I could tell right away that he really wasn't prepared when the three of us sat down for an introduction, John with his gel-spiked jet-black hair and rosy-cheeked smile, looking not many years older than my guys. He was in fact thirty-six but had a childlike hopefulness and relentlessly upbeat attitude that I later described as puppylike. He'd been president of one of the other fraternities on Nineteenth Avenue, had played baseball professionally, and had owned a bar near campus most recently—all experiences that Rod thought made him a perfect fit for our account.

And it's true that John instantly bonded with the guys, often much to my annoyance as he gave them advice that was contrary to mine, explaining how to juggle the demands of several girls at once and cheering them right on about their idiotic drinking games. He was very definitely one of the boys and I thought of him as one more member of that year's pledge class. But his experience of frat life had not included the kind of dining experience I was offering and he seemed to have been hired more for his social skills than for his food knowledge.

Obviously fresh from corporate food-training camp, he made his first pitch to me apparently unaware that I had just returned from my own kind of summer camp ready to churn my own butter and cure duck breasts and culture cream in the basement. "Microwavable macaroni and cheese packets," he repeated when I uttered a rhetorical "*what?*" after he explained that he was in a sales competition to unload the most product and was targeting frat boys as the ideal market. "Your guys could win a Wii!" he cajoled when I seemed less than enthusiastic, receiving the response that I would rather buy my guys ten Wii's with my own money than serve that crap. And in the background, I could hear Rod laughing, fully aware of the dragon's den he'd sent his green new guy into. Soon after, he called to ask if he could bring a broker to meet me and sample precooked salmon, to which I responded, "This is Seattle." I thought I was clear enough, but that being too subtle a no, I had to walk him through it: "You take something that is fresh and local and requires eight minutes cooking time and you replace it with a frozen mummified product from China that requires twenty minutes to reheat. Who would ever buy that?" And I learned that the sort of bar and grill that serves cheap cocktails and beer in plastic cups is the place to avoid the salmon burger.

But Rod had not assigned John to me as punishment, something I realized when he made a request of me: "Sometime, could you tell him that you're planning a special meal and you want his suggestions? Just see how he responds." It wasn't that he wanted me to test so much as to teach and unlike a lot of others in the food industry similarly ignorant of the product they were selling, John asked questions and seemed genuinely interested in the answers. He watched me butcher chickens, expressing surprise that wings came from there, as if the fried and hot-sauced thing you got at a sports bar were another sort of animal altogether. He watched me spoon melted fat out of a pan of brisket and asked what I intended to do with it. He was surprised that I was throwing it in the trash, as if the fat should be headed for a second life in a soup. And he queried me about things I thought were common knowledge, like the difference between evaporated and condensed milk. He was amazed that when you drizzled oil into eggs you got mayonnaise and that a few more ingredients turned it into Caesar dressing. So I didn't mind that he didn't know much about the subject because he was curious in a way that made me look at food from perspectives I'd never thought of.

John came to us at just the time the House took a leap to eighty members, making ours a more lucrative account than when I'd started with a group of fifty. The rush chairs had told me this with great excitement, expecting me to share in the joy and not understanding that this was not good news to me. So to cope, I hired restaurant critic Leslie Kelly, whom I'd met at the farm, to assist in the kitchen while also writing articles for *Serious Eats*, part of a series on her journey as "critic-turned-cook." She had already written about her experiences at such well-known Seattle restaurants as Dahlia Lounge and

Delancey, and when she told prolific restaurateur and James Beard Award–winning chef Tom Douglas that her next stop was a frat house, he had rolled his eyes.

I had always strived for the respect and approval of those in my direct professional circle, the vendors and service people I dealt with every day, so when she told me about the Douglas comment, I'd not only been irritated by the cliché assumptions behind it, but I was also personally pissed and wanted to make a statement. So I gave her tasks like preparing Thai curry paste from scratch and squeezing oranges for balsamic vinaigrette and one day we made chicken cordon bleu, starting with the pounding of eighty chicken breasts and ending with our hands caked in flour, milk, and eggs. I wrote REAL CHICKEN CORDON BLEU on the posted menu, prompting one of the guys to ask with complete seriousness if I ever served fake chicken. It was the last time I made something requiring the labor of two people for four solid hours.

Leslie stopped working at the House after fall quarter and while I missed the extra hands, I didn't miss the mental exhaustion of being a nonstop foodie show-off. But I continued to aim for authenticity, one day making pho starting with the butchering of a dozen chickens, which reminded me that the night before I had dreamed I was carving up live human beings—my guys, in fact—the way I'd fabricated the goat at Quillisascut. "A lot of work for soup," I grumbled to some of the guys hanging out in the kitchen, but there I was doing it without any of them holding a gun to my head.

But even if the guys weren't forcing me into this, they were increasingly supportive, food issues becoming part of the college curriculum. I knew this when pledge Jacob, whose academically gifted older brother had been in the House and who was himself a promising engineering major not on my radar as a food activist, gave me a copy of the *Food, Inc.* workbook he was finished with. And freshman Richard, whom I'd stopped calling Little Dick about the same time I realized how big he was destined to be in my world, brought me a KNOW THE INGREDIENTS sticker to hang in the kitchen. Pledge Mitch told me that Michael Pollan was on the reading list of his political science class, and when Bob started sending me links to articles about food recalls and guys I knew to be conservative were using terms like "sustainable" and "grass-fed," I knew this was an entirely different audience than I had started with: an audience that still ate garbage when I wasn't around, but wanted to know if the milk I was buying was hormone-free.

Even Badley used his new power to try to steer the course of food service his way, issuing edicts that I routinely ignored, despite sometimes agreeing with him in principle. He would send me emails with subject headings like, "We should eat more of these," with a link to a *New York Times* article listing anchovies and beets as miracle foods, which I loved myself but which some of the pickier eaters referred to as flatworms and dirt. And he declared that onions should be banned, but mussels and duck breast should make more regular appearances. When he sensed that I was tuning him out, he'd send a freshman in to request things that obviously had the president's imprimatur, things like, "I was just wondering if you could put capers in the tuna salad, but no red onion." It wasn't just the specificity of the requests; it was that the freshmen were so terrified of me that they'd make breadless sandwiches rather than come ask me for a loaf. So I could spot this form of hazing the minute I saw a hesitant pledge standing in the kitchen about to make a request.

Even without Badley's helpful suggestions, I was rethinking the menu, determining that I didn't have to give up gyros and Philly cheesesteaks just because I had banned the oddly uniform chunks of manipulated frozen meat. There were ways of getting those same crave-inducing flavors without making myself insane trying to re-create the look of something invented in a lab. So I tried new things like ground lamb with Indian spices rolled into naan and Greek-inspired chicken wraps. And recalling the beef po'boys of my New Orleans childhood, I braised chuck roast for several hours, shredding it and serving it with sliced baguettes. I set these out one Friday when I noticed Riley standing by the cereal dispensers pulling every last scrap of dried strawberries out of a bowl of Special K before sitting down to eat cereal while his pledge brothers dug into the hot beef sandwiches. It was Big Dick who said what I was thinking.

It wasn't that Riley didn't like good food and it wasn't even that he was picky the way Perry had been. "It's a texture thing," he had told Big Dick in that comic book character voice he would put on when challenged about anything. He pulled all of the dried strawberries out because they got revoltingly spongy in a weird way when you put the milk on them. He was right when I thought about it, so I eventually dropped them from my order not only because of the suspicious strawberries but also because of the high fructose corn syrup. It was texture, too, that explained Riley's love of lettuce sandwiches, a favorite I learned about when I put two heads of green leaf out on the lunch table one day and found the bowl empty within an hour. "It's Riley," they told me. I didn't believe it until I saw him myself one day with nothing but four inches of lettuce between two slices of white bread.

"Crunchy," he had said in explanation of why everyone else in line was out of luck on the lettuce front.

Riley might have been a challenge, but pledge Charlie called my bacon-wrapped cambozola-stuffed figs "little orbs of ecstasy" on Facebook. And pledge Watson, known to be the food connoisseur of that freshman group, asked for my recipes for Grits with Goat Cheese and "that butternut squash thing." And although they had been around the year before, it was not until this year that I met the ladies I came to call the food bandits, a group of sorority girls who would sneak into the House for leftovers.

Most of what I knew about sororities and the sisters who lived in them was secondhand. But when I did see a girl in the House, she was almost certainly from one of a couple of sororities the guys closely associated with. Just as the guys formed bonds with a big bro and little bro, they would adopt a big sis and little sis, and these pretend clans would get together for Family Night, hanging out for movies and pizza. It was a touching arrangement spoiled occasionally when one of the guys would ruin the dynamic by sleeping with his sis. And usually when I was introduced to a girl, it was as the pretend sibling of one of my guys, or more rarely, as his serious girlfriend. But in general these young women were simply not around during the hours that I worked.

The previous year I had started receiving notes left overnight: "We love Darlene's yummy food," "Alpha Sigma Phi boys love Darlene," and "We love you and stuffed bell peppers!" I suppose it should have been obvious to me that no guy was the author of those notes, but it wasn't until this year when one was signed by Dagney and Taylor, and I knew there were no such people in the House, that I realized I had sorority groupies. I couldn't help thinking of Goldilocks when I heard about their late-night sessions, except that for these girls everything at this House was always just right, which I guess wasn't surprising since I later learned that theirs was a steady diet of "chicken with shit on it." "Just chicken," Dagney explained helpfully when I finally met her. "And then some kind of shit on it." "A different kind every day," Taylor added, as if that slightly improved matters.

Having outed themselves, I expected to hear their review when I sent cornbread as the Alpha Sig contribution to a dinner their house was hosting and received it in Taylor's happy red handwriting on my whiteboard the morning after. "What does 'jizz-worthy' mean?" I asked sophomore Patrick when I read the note, assuming that the three exclamation points were a good sign. "The cornbread was jizz-worthy!!!" they'd declared. Patrick was one of several California imports whose family owned a winery, a fact he was so modest about that I didn't know it until he was about to graduate and he gave me a bottle from his family business. He was one of those wealthy people with the class and breeding to shut up about it and it was only when I asked him if he'd ever watched *The Real Housewives of Orange County* and he told me that he *knew* some of the housewives of Orange County that I suspected he wasn't fretting over student aid. Patrick, who at the time was not public about being gay, was obviously uncomfortable about the "jizzy" question, explaining that a bunch of young women found similarities between sheet pans of quick bread and orgasm. But he didn't put it quite that way. "Um," he said, shifting on the kitchen stool long enough for me to wish I hadn't asked. "It means they found it similar to a pleasurable physical sensation." And I could tell that he was greatly relieved that I could do a mental translation of this and break the pregnant moment with, "Oh. Well. Who knew?"

It was wonderful to have the support of these high-spirited young women, validating in a different way than what I had from the guys because they were making an active choice to seek out this food. And I adored them even when I learned that it wasn't just my scratch cooking they were pilfering. "When no one's looking, they take bags of cereal and throw them out the kitchen window and come back for them later," one of the guys told me when I protested about the alarming rate at which they were running through granola. "Girls gone food wild!" I mocked and I might have looked more harshly on this if it weren't that enough of the guys knew about it that they could have prevented it if they wanted to. It was common knowledge that the houses stole from each other, but it was usually furniture or photographs or anything with Greek letters. I learned about this when I saw Bob instructing our carpenter, Ross, to bolt the class composite photographs to the wall, lest the girls make off with 1967 or 1985.

Whether it was food or fraternity memorabilia theft, the police ignored these pranks and took a similar hands-off approach to almost everything else that went on in the community save for acts of violence. Even gross stupidity was met with a fair level of tolerance as Badley learned the year when cops knocked on the door to tell him to "get those two idiots off the roof or we'll cite you with a noise violation," the two idiots being freshmen in postexam euphoria. That same month, several of the pledges paid a visit to Dick's Drive-In, where their behavior was enough to have them forcibly removed from the premises, the manager calling the SPD for good measure. Fortunately it was Riley who was driving so that when the cops pulled up behind him at the House, they discovered a sober driver with three passengers so plastered they couldn't remember why they'd arrived home without the burgers they'd set out for. The officers could have cited all four as minors in possession, but characteristically they let it go, presumably as a reward for Riley's sobriety behind the wheel. So it was all the more startling when I learned one morning in December that police in riot gear had used pepper spray against students on Seventeenth Avenue.

The night before, there'd been a power outage affecting all of the fraternities and sororities and the residents had responded like crazed sports hooligans, lighting bonfires in the street and refusing to disperse. It was the sort of stupid and rash thing that rarely happened, but that the press would focus on as if it defined the Greek system; you never read about the fund-raisers, let alone the more private moments of generosity within the houses. But while everyone else had lost their minds along with the power, Richard was in the attic with a flashlight where the storm had blown off a portion of the roof and single-handedly spent the next four hours installing tarp over the hole. Naturally there was nothing about that in the *Seattle Times* the next day, just the image of drunken buffoons dancing around a burning couch.

That night Richard had spontaneously taken on what should have been the house manager's job, but the holder of that position had broken his Achilles heel trying to climb into his third-floor window from the second-floor deck. So while it was generally true that the freshmen were like baboons suddenly liberated from the zoo, Richard had never needed the older guys to house-train him and was in fact considerably more responsible than most of them. Blair, too, quickly established which of the brothers to respect and which to ignore, and revealed himself as haze-proof when his response to a sophomore's bullying was to tell him that he didn't really feel like making himself sick right that moment, but that he might decide to do that later on under his own initiative. "Just not right now while your fat ass is yelling at me," he had communicated without actually saying the words.

That self-assuredness and nonconformity was what made him my Care Blair, hanging out in the kitchen to cheer me on in my battles. "Do you make your suppliers give you what you want?" he had asked me one day. He'd asked the question after witnessing my second rejection in a row of a shipment of Asian Gold chemically treated shrimp instead of the wild domestic product I'd been promised and the subsequent call to my new sales guy, John, who was unavailable to talk to me because he was in a seminar. What sort of seminar I didn't know, but I commented to Blair that it better be the one on How to Respond to the Customer Who Vomits the Toxic Contents of Her Brain into Your Head. And when I later learned that it was one of author Jeffrey Gitomer's lectures, in which he advises on avoiding negative people and situations, I thought, you just cannot make this stuff up. John finally addressed the matter with his seafood buyer by explaining that "this customer is very particular about her shrimp," and I wondered how many adjectives he'd spun through his head before settling on "particular." But, no, I told Blair; I can't make them give me what I want when all the more important customers were perfectly happy to buy products with a shelf life of twenty years.

When I couldn't get what I wanted, I would resort to making what I wanted before I would bend to John's suggestions of "a really nice product." He would say this to me in a way that made me certain he genuinely believed in the niceness of his products and was not just being a salesman, which bothered me more. That February, it was crepes that I wanted for the Mother-Son Brunch, and because I couldn't obtain the kind that were just flour, eggs, and milk, I stood in my home kitchen on the prior Saturday making two hundred of them for smoked salmon tortes. I wanted to be able to tell the moms I'd slaved for hours on my day off as well as spending another day off serving them brunch, even if I wasn't actually going to tell them that and even if none of them expected me to crucify myself for their sake and probably wouldn't have minded if I *had* served one of John's really nice products.

It was the second year the Parents' Club had held a Mother-Son Brunch and it sounded lovely in principle, except that in practice, it meant that the moms worked hard at planning, organizing, inviting, setting up, and shopping while the guys largely sat back and enjoyed a Sunday meal, some sneaking the mimosas intended for the ladies. And because it was on the weekend, I was in the House every day for twelve days straight by the Friday after the event. I wasn't resentful of this on day one and enjoyed the challenge of serving my crepe tortes and roasted shrimp platters on the seventh day. But by day twelve, I was on the edge when I came into the kitchen and discovered the dining hall looking like a bomb had detonated and Riley cleaning and making it plain that he wasn't there by choice, spewing a stream of wildly sarcastic commentary on how much he was enjoying himself, which might have been funny if I'd had a weekend break.

I put the potatoes and chopped onions and peppers on the stove and began to sauté them for a hash and pulled out eggs to bake on top. As I was doing this, Riley had gained an audience to cheer on his act and having had enough and just wanting peace, I closed the door between the kitchen and the show. And that's when it really got ugly, Riley finding it hilarious that he'd pushed me to the edge and just wanting to push that little bit more. It was when he got to "she's on her way out, I'm on my way up" that I opened the door and said, "You want me out; you got it." And I left bacon in the oven and raw eggs and my House keys on the counter and walked out. It was almost two weeks later that he presented me with a letter of apology that the leadership team ordered him to write as his punishment, although the wording was clearly his own. But by then I had moved on to being pissed off about at least a dozen other things having nothing to do with him, and I smiled when I read it, telling him that I'd completely let it go.

Occasionally I would pull up craigslist to remind myself that almost every other food service job was much worse than mine, with laughable pay, horrible hours, and less colorful customers. But I still found myself standing over the compost bin insanely contemplating throwing myself in to be devoured by the fruit flies, so shortly after "the Riley incident" as it became known, I counted the hours until my husband and I were headed to Vietnam for spring break.

We had applied for a visa a couple of months earlier when it dawned on us that a communist country probably required one, and we spent the week in Ho Chi Minh City, formerly and still commonly known as Saigon, where it seemed like everyone ate constantly and well, despite the obvious poverty. Everywhere we went, all day long, there was something grilling or frying right on the street—all of it fresh from the market and filling the air with the scent of cilantro and mint, lime and toasted sesame oil. And we found a local coffee chain, Highlands, that reminded us of home, learning later from Bob that its founder had grown up in Seattle and returned to his birthplace in the nineties to start a company inspired by Starbucks. He had also been a member of Alpha Sigma Phi.

It seemed that no matter where I went in the world, I could never get away from my guys, but I returned rested and inspired, adding Pork Meatball Banh Mi to my repertoire, to the delight of John, who made a point of arriving around lunchtime on the days it appeared on the menu. He would happily eat a Taco Bell burrito and then surprise me by being open to the strange offerings from my kitchen, even the exotic new Vietnamese sandwich with the slightly dirty-sock smell of fish sauce. And he was there shortly after I returned when I asked if he could sense that the Buddhism had seeped in and he asked if I was on medication before telling me that actually he'd never minded being assigned to this account and didn't find me to be a problem customer at all. But being John, he couldn't just leave it at that and went on for several minutes about how it didn't bother him to see my name flash on his phone and how he didn't wince at the sight of an email from me, not one bit. And then he put the cherry on top by assuring me that when he talked to his boss, Rod, about me, he didn't ever call me a bitch, not ever.

Late in the year, when I had had most of the idealism of the prior summer farm experience beaten out of me, Rod arranged a meeting with his boss, a VP of sales, to talk to me about chicken from Draper Valley Farms in Richard's hometown in the Skagit Valley, and to introduce a new program with a natural meat supplier out of Eugene, Oregon. The date of the meeting was chosen by their people, which probably explains why no one stopped to consider the wisdom of scheduling a serious discussion on the day after Cinco de Mayo at a frat house. "Can you make sure we have a reasonably clean place to sit?" I asked Richard, who by now was not just playing house manager, but had become his assistant.

When we met, Rod's boss told me that his company had sponsored *Jamie Oliver's Food Revolution*, a televised attempt to rid schools of processed crap, which was sort of like telling me the National Rifle Association had sponsored a yoga retreat, the kind of news that you have a hard time wrapping your brain around. But I was skeptical and went ahead with my demonstration of two chicken breasts. One was from the unidentified mass-production facility somewhere far to the east and looked like it had gone through a wood chipper, and one was from Draper just up the road and was not only plumper and richer in color, but was also covered in skin that didn't appear to have been chewed on by a coyote. "What do you have against Arkansas?" Rod had teased as I finished my show-and-tell, but his boss told me there was no reason why it needed to be so hard to get me what I wanted when it was so close, which is exactly what I'd been saying forever.

The year ended with the graduations of the guys I'd met as doe-eyed pledges on my first day of work. For many of them there was little out there beyond low-paying service jobs, most having majored in fields on the bottom end of the demand scale. Some continued to work in the same dead-end restaurant jobs they'd held through college, and some hopefully shoved their foot into whatever door they could. Newman and Jesse took positions with a promising start-up company. And Badley went to Washington to intern with Senator Murray. "It's not a job if you don't get paid," Newman had quipped when I remarked on Badley's good fortune by exclaiming, "A 2010 graduate with a *job*!"

It was harder to see that group graduate than any before them, but except for Badley, most of them had already been pulling away by living on their own. And in some ways, I had moved on without actually leaving. I had thought that I should probably graduate at the end of four years, too, but when the time actually came, I knew there was still a lot left to achieve. And although I had thought no one could quite replace that original group, there'd been new faces this year that I wanted to see in the next. There'd been freshmen who seemed to know that macaroni and cheese shouldn't glow in the dark, even if they secretly ate it when I wasn't looking, and vendors who seemed to be meeting me at least halfway without such a struggle. And there was that thing that was always there: Where else would I go? Who else would have me?

Blueberry Cornbread

The blueberries are optional, but great.

FOR 1 10-INCH CAST-IRON SKILLET, SERVING 6–8 PEOPLE:

4 T. butter
1½ cups medium- or coarse-grain cornmeal
½ cup flour
1½ tsp. baking powder
1 tsp. salt
6 T. sugar
2 eggs
1¼ cups whole milk
1½ cups fresh or frozen blueberries

Place butter in a 10-inch cast-iron skillet and place in a 375-degree oven until butter is melted. Stir together cornmeal, flour, baking powder, salt, and sugar. In a separate bowl, beat eggs and stir in milk. Add liquid ingredients to dry ingredients, stir in blueberries, and pour mixture into the hot skillet. Bake 30 minutes and serve with butter and honey.

11

Progress

"Canned food is a perversion," Ignatius said. *"I suspect that it is ultimately very damaging to the soul."*
—JOHN KENNEDY TOOLE, *A CONFEDERACY OF DUNCES*

Before I returned to the Alpha Sig House for a fifth year, I saw my doctor for a routine checkup. "How's your work-related stress level?" he asked me as he reviewed my file, as though it indicated my profession were air traffic controller or bomb disabler. "Any feelings of being over-whelmed? Hopelessness? Thoughts of suicide?" he asked as if seriously expecting an affirmative response on all counts. When he got to "how's your breathing," I answered that I still was and wondered if the psych ward at Virginia Mason had seen a spike in frat house cooks ready to end it all over one more goddamn overripe banana fight on the dining hall floor. But while I knew my thoughts might turn fleetingly to homicide in the coming weeks, self-destruction was not on my mind; I'd spent part of my summer in a learning experience that made me grateful for what I had, cars in my parking spot and exploded beer cans in my freezer notwithstanding, and I returned more empowered than ever.

Trying to recapture some of the inspiration I'd gained on the farm, I took a three-week job at a preschool, vacation relief for the regular cook. The connection between this and my regular work seemed completely obvious to me, even if the guys wondered what I could possibly learn from the palates of four-year-olds. But if the farm had reconnected me to food, this experience reminded me of how completely joyless it could be when the cook was stuck with USDA regulations so specific and rigid that they squeezed out any fun you could have in preparing—let alone eating—the "½ cup milk, fluid" and the "½ slice bread or bread alternate, including ⅓ cup cereal, cold, dry." Reading the rules reminded me of those horrible American Cancer Society cookbooks that made you want to die of starvation instead.

And it wasn't just the government straitjacket and lack of quality ingredients that got to me. After four years at the Alpha Sig House, I had become hardened and wildly profane, but here at the preschool every morning I would read signs like the one urging all of us to BE KIND EVEN WHEN YOU ARE FEELING ICKY. "I have to be sweet and I can't swear my head off," I told Rod, who thought this was as funny as if you sent me away without access to email or red wine, and looked forward to the possibility that the exercise in civility might have some lasting effect. And while I did not get what I wanted out of the experience, I did gain a new appreciation for the enormous freedom I had at my regular job and returned inspired.

But before that, I spent some of the summer in New

Orleans and was not there more than a day before a reminder that work/life balance meant something entirely different to my customers, namely that their lives were my work. I was sitting at Café Du Monde in the French Quarter enjoying café au lait and beignets with my husband and my mother and two sons when I received a text from Badley, who'd just begun his internship in DC. "Can you send me a recipe for a super tasty and fancy cookie that I could make for my intern potluck? Key phrase is 'that I could make.'" I replied that I was on vacation, but it didn't seem to register. "Okay, well just let me know. There's a girl here I'm trying to impress." When the third text came, my husband was giving me that look.

He was a great supporter of what I was trying to achieve with these guys, but it still wore on him at times the way I'm sure it would wear on me if his customers were constantly sending him requests for computer advice while we were sipping cocktails. "She's a vegetarian, so no bacon cookies," he wrote, referring to a twist on peanut butter cookies I had made when I was finally able to obtain pork I wasn't ashamed of. So I sent him a link to Dorie Greenspan's slightly salty and deeply dark chocolate World Peace Cookies, which seemed like the right thing for a senatorial internship party.

Shortly after I returned to Seattle, several of the guys attended an Alpha Sig gathering in the city I'd just left and I received a shouted voice mail from the new house president, Nick: "I'm here in New Orleans with Johnny and Richard and Blodgett and Corey and we were thinking of you and wondering where to eat." Richard, who was to be the new house manager, sent me a text asking the same question. And I told them to go to Cochon, which they did, remarking for months afterward about the experience and inquiring as to when fried alligator might make an appearance on my menus. It was a rare week in any summer that I didn't hear from at least one of the guys, if only to make sure I was still there.

I had wanted to meet the whole leadership team for lunch before the school year began, but only Bob and treasurer Corey could make it, the others trying to work every remaining hour to pay for some portion of their growing student debt. I had been reluctant to return without meaningful help in the kitchen and so Corey nominated an absent Blair for the job because "A, he needs the money, and B, he gets along with you." You could say the same for lots of the guys on the A part, but the way Corey said the B portion, you'd have thought that Blair had some kind of specialized training. Reassuringly the text I got from Blair later showed no indication at all that he felt forcibly drafted: "I see you're looking for a sous chef?! That sounds like my dream job!"

Before we ordered, I pulled out an article in the paper about how processed-food manufacturers were using up salmonella-laced eggs, arguing that it was a perfectly fine thing since cooking destroyed the pathogen. I hated the way industrial food companies used this "shut up and eat it" tone, a phrase that I myself felt perfectly justified using on my guys. We had just come through what I came to call the summer of the rat shit eggs, a massive national recall of salmonella-tainted eggs from a "farm" in the Midwest that was really a concrete chicken prison. I had been moving away from large industrial food slowly, but the images of chickens crammed together in warehouses feasting on rat feces galvanized me to immediately stop buying eggs from my regular food distributor and to seek out a local source from free-range chickens.

Tom the dairyman was happy to supply me both with milk that hadn't been heated to flavor-killing ultra-pasteurized temperatures and eggs from a Washington farm.

"You can have white or brown," he offered. And in one breathless sentence he went on, "They're the same in terms of nutrition, but the sorority girls think the brown ones are healthier; don't even get me started on the sororities." And then he told me I had a choice of regular, free-range, and organic. I was confused by the options and confirmed that they were all from the same farm. "So they have different levels of happiness for their chickens?" I asked. And he affirmed that indeed some were living a better life than others on the same property. I couldn't help think that it was just like that at the Alpha Sig House, where the pledges were the regular and the seniors were the organic. But when I looked at my first case, I noticed that the box proudly claimed that "ALL of our chickens are given a nutritious diet free of antibiotics or hormones, raised with shelter, resting areas, sufficient space, and the ability to engage in natural behaviors," that latter euphemism being particularly relevant to a place where even the pledges seemed to be doing okay in the "natural behaviors" department.

A month into the school year, the walk-in refrigerator I'd demanded as a condition for my return arrived in pieces that some of the construction management majors had promised to assemble. The Board had agreed to the $8,000 price tag after much lobbying from me, and Bob had reluctantly allowed me to use a precious space in the basement covered in tiles paid for and inscribed with the names of alumni. "Do you really care?" I had asked some of the more senior alumni when they'd been at the House for Founders' Day the year before and they'd agreed that Bob should give me whatever I wanted.

I knew when I ordered it that it would be seven feet in height, but what I hadn't taken into account was that we needed at least a foot of clearance for ventilation and the area in question had a lower ceiling height than the rest of the basement. There was nowhere else to put it and so as I stood there with my helpers, Martel and Trevor, and our handyman, Ross, with the unassembled panels of my new toy—a little stressed about my possibly catastrophic mistake—I looked up at the ceiling and asked the same question they had as we all realized that the outdoor deck was directly above us. So we might have to create a little raised area up there, but we at least wouldn't need to saw into anyone's bedroom. I was in the kitchen when I heard the heaving grunts of several of the guys lifting the vent onto the finished unit and Martel and Trevor came to tell me that there was maybe a pencil-width clearance.

I was thrilled that I no longer had to stuff my refrigerators or leave chicken sitting out at just the moment the health inspector visited, but I was afraid to close the door when I went in, the thing being in the basement where the guys only went for evening beer pong and Thursday night parties. I realized it was irrational, but the fear persisted until Blair suggested I confront my terror by entering and closing the door while he stood outside. And it was as we were playing this game that I noticed the YOU ARE NOT LOCKED IN sign on the interior and discovered that even if some sick little bastard decided to lock me in, there was a knob to turn that forced the lock to fall to the ground. We tried it out several times, taking turns and laughing hysterically as we watched the locking mechanism fall to pieces each time. But Blair was nonchalant about even a remote possibility of being trapped inside, reasoning that it was a fridge and not a freezer and suggesting that I just keep a blanket in there.

When I looked back at all the forms of kitchen help I'd had over the years, the happiest, if not the most productive, were the two quarters that Blair worked for me, separated by the quarter he spent in Ecuador. He began as a sophomore in the fall of this, my fifth year, and was reasonably reliable. By this I mean that when he was "sick," he would ask me for permission to be late or if he had the foresight to know in advance he was just thinking about being "sick" he would clear it with me. He also knew that he could get off work by invoking some school-related matter like a quiz to study for or a paper to finish, and I didn't question this. Although I did inquire into why the three hours he was supposed to give me were less important than the three incriminating hours from the night before captured on Facebook.

He never mastered the art of working while talking and would put his knife down and tell a story for ten minutes, all the while being paid by the hour, and he had the most annoying aversions to certain textures and sounds so that when he poured cold chicken stock into freezer bags, you'd think he was being nailed to the cross for all the lamentation. He would almost vomit at the thought of running his finger along the rim of the whipping cream container to get the stubborn thickest part out.

But he was funny and fiercely loyal to me, so I tolerated a lot, even his incessant tweets like, "My boss just told me to fuck off, is that legal?" And "I know workplace harassment when it hits me in the face by a woman half my size." And he was interested in a broad range of subjects, constantly asking questions, not just of me but of guys passing through the kitchen, so it was completely in character for him to forgo the usual forms of pledge persecution by requiring them to answer questions about themselves to gain his signature, something the pledges had to get from each of the brothers:

> *For Blair's signature, list the following:*
> 10 favorite movies
> 9 things you want to do before you die
> 8 places you want to visit
> 7 things you want to learn how to do
> 6 favorite TV shows
> 5 sports you like/want to play
> 4 places you want to live
> 3 positions you might run for in the House
> 2 bad habits of yours
> 1 favorite place to eat
> *Must be written neatly. No bullshit answers. No repeat answers.*

AT THE BEGINNING OF every year, I felt a need to do something novel to inspire me and this year I decided that installing a Magnetic Poetry board on the kitchen door would help channel my creative energy in a positive direction. I had intended this for my use, but I knew that some of the guys would contribute and so I avoided the kits labeled EROTIC and SEXUAL INNUENDO, and ordered the ostensibly safe FOOD WORDS KIT. It wasn't long before one of them reminded me that there is no boundary I can erect that they cannot surmount:

I TASTE THE SUCCULENT SAUCE & DRIZZLE
THICK RICH CREAM ON MY PORK AND FEEL
AN ORGANIC PASSION TO EAT YOUR FEAST.
YOU SATISFY TONGUES AND
FILL MOUTHS

But because I was never the sort of parent to install blocking
software on my kids' computers or tell them who their friends
could be, I left the board in place and found myself standing
in front of it awkwardly when parents and VIPs would visit
to spare them the call to SEAR MY COLD CARROT WITH YOUR
SIMMERING OYSTER, or the observation that SHE WOULD SAVOR
BITTER BITES OF HIS SUCCULENT ENDIVE LIKE MOIST SAUSAGE.

I had been ambivalent about returning, as I was pretty much
every September; after a summer of lunching with friends and
idle blackberry picking and cooking for two, it was hard to return to a rigid schedule and the unglamorous physical toil. But
on my first day back, a bouquet of flowers and a bottle of wine
sat on my worktable next to a handwritten sign: HERE'S TO AN-
OTHER GREAT YEAR. WE ARE SO LUCKY TO HAVE YOU. And sorority girl Taylor, one of the food bandits, peeked into the
kitchen to say, "I love you. I just wanted you to know that,"
with that sort of adoring gaze your newborn gives you, which
you try to remember when he's sixteen and storming out of the
house telling you he hates you. Whatever horribleness was
ahead, I knew I could think back to these notes and I love you's;
it was the promise of all of that that held me, year after year.

On John's first visit of the school year, he told me that another of his customers who'd heard of me had asked if I was
crazy. And John, being the sort of refreshingly honest salesman
who seemed to have missed company lectures on bullshitting

the customer, told me that he'd replied, "Well, not *crazy* crazy." But if my relentless pursuit of real food and thoughtful sourcing had been out of the mainstream when I'd begun four years earlier, I was starting to see signs of hope. With smug satisfaction, I received an email from Rod linking me to the National Restaurant Association's prediction for the top ten food trends for 2011, seven of ten of which I had been restlessly promoting for years:

1. Locally sourced meat and seafood
2. Locally grown produce
3. Sustainability
4. Nutritionally balanced children's dishes
5. Hyperlocal (restaurant gardens, do your own butchery)
6. Children's nutrition
7. Sustainable seafood
8. Gluten-free/allergy conscious
9. Simplicity/back to basics
10. Farm/estate-branded ingredients

Still, it seemed that whenever I discovered one of his company's products that met my standards, it had a life expectancy of about six months. When I complained about this to Rod, he would look up sales data and share the depressing news that "I'm showing we only moved two cases of that in the past two months. And I can guess who the purchaser was." I could be totally in the right, but if the chains and corporate restaurants weren't buying, it didn't matter. And when I suggested it was all a conspiracy against me, Rod laughed. "Yeah, corporate keeps a list of all the product you like so we know what to discontinue," which I didn't think was entirely a joke.

The power of the big food manufacturers was such that when I served a cake with buttercream frosting, surprisingly consisting of butter and cream, the guys were confused by the taste. I served it on October 11, unaware that it was Riley's birthday. And Riley, who was so particular about everything he put in his mouth, beamed as he helped himself to a large piece as if it had been made just for him. But some of the guys, while enjoying it, asked what was on top and told me that it didn't taste like "normal" icing.

Real Vanilla Frosting

FOR ABOUT 6 CUPS:

Combine together in an electric mixer:

12 oz. butter, at room temperature
½ cup cream
1 T. vanilla
2 lbs. powdered sugar
a pinch of salt

It was enough for the guys who'd originally hired me that I served meat you could identify as something other than road-kill, but by my fifth year, there was an appetite for things that surprised even me, things like tongue and sweetbreads, neither of which seemed likely to be popular enough to add to the menu. But the food at this House was sufficiently notorious by now that you could expect just about anything. I was working on what I thought was a completely safe choice one day when I heard several of the guys murmuring about a "weird" dinner. I wondered why baked penne was so controversial, until I saw Brian standing in front of my handwritten menu and then turning to ask me if they were really about to eat baked beaver. And I realized in that moment that I had so transformed the food that rather than assuming poor penmanship, the guys believed a large aquatic rodent was a new addition to an ever-expanding diet.

"You mean the critter that builds dams?" Kevin asked when I let the misunderstanding go. "With the tail, and all that . . ." he added, his voice trailing off. "A little gamey," I confessed, and he asked me if that was even legal. When I'd had enough of the murmured complaints, I yelled out to those gathered in the dining hall that "you are *not* eating beaver tonight!" It was one of those statements you only think better of after it's too late. Several months later, I had obviously failed again to clearly write "penne," and Jake asked me flatly, with neither humor nor revulsion, if they were really having penis for dinner. "Nose to tail," I decided to answer. "It's what I'm all about." And he seemed to just accept that: roast chicken last night, penis tonight, without asking what I thought was the most obvious question.

That October, a family crisis brought Badley back to Seattle briefly and he came to the House as a surprise dinner guest. He showed me pictures of the cookies he'd made to impress the girl, which looked nothing at all like the recipe I had sent him; they should have been jet black, where his were pale golden

with flecks of brown, a cookie suspiciously resembling a recipe from the back of a chocolate chip bag. But he insisted they
were exactly what I'd told him to do, despite the photograph
proving otherwise, which was so like him.

Guest speakers at Chapter Dinner were usually older
alumni, successful men invited to motivate and inspire, which
I thought should be interspersed with *un*successful men to
motivate in a different sort of way, although I wasn't sure
how that invitation would go: "We've reached our quota of
winners in the game of life, so we were wondering if you were
available next Monday?" When his internship with Senator
Murray ended, Badley had taken a job with a lobbying firm,
one of its major customers being Sara Lee, which he knew I
would view about as favorably as if they represented a chewing tobacco company. And while I was glad that he at least
had a paycheck, I knew he'd started at the very bottom when
he texted me to ask where he could buy bus tubs for a party
his company was hosting. So when he spoke that Monday in
October, he advised the undergraduates to join the military,
disillusioned with having spent four years in college to forage
around DC restaurant supply stores. But he went back to
Washington, determined if less idealistic, and I thought about
him when I would see some from more privileged backgrounds
squandering their advantages and going nowhere in life, or
others from equally difficult backgrounds who blamed their
present on their past.

With Halloween approaching, Blair planned to dress as
David Beckham to Taylor's Victoria, but was having a hard
time reaching recent graduate Jesse, who owned the necessary
costume. It seemed a small matter to me, but he went on
about it for days, stopping whatever kitchen task he was

assigned to fret about how he couldn't just wear any old soccer jersey. The Halloween cruise on Lake Union, which never seemed to go well and one year ended in a bloody fight that saw one member removed from the fraternity and everyone banned by the cruise line the following year, was back on the calendar. And all the guys but Blair seemed to be having the kind of giddy fun with the buildup that I hadn't seen since my kids were about five.

Kevin went into character, pulling on a pair of tights, wearing a paper crown, waving a limp scepter he'd created out of cardboard, and asking me what you call a cape when it's on a king. Carlos and Ryan donned cowboy hats, gingham shirts, and toy guns and called me Mama Darlene, and Chris settled for his usual afternoon attire of a bathrobe, content to call it a costume even if everyone else called it lame. But when Blair had not secured the appropriate dress by 3:00 P.M. on cruise day, I told him to just get himself to Goodwill and throw together a pirate outfit. "That doesn't make any sense," he had protested, worried about having to explain all night why Victoria Beckham was out on the town with Jack Sparrow. And Carlos, exasperated with what he saw as the real issue, Blair's overconcern with what people think, suggested that he meet all inquiries with a self-confident, "I'm the pirate screwing Victoria Beckham. Who the hell are you?" But just in time, a beaming Blair appeared in the kitchen and turned his back to me so I could see the lettering BECKHAM.

Fall quarter was always the more traditional and formal part of the year and dinner guests in the past had included UW president Mark Emmert, who soon went on to become president of the NCAA. The chief of police had eaten here and a prominent defense attorney, who had no problem holding the guys' attention, unlike some speakers with less immediately relevant material than what not to do or say when arrested. I always wondered what these VIP guests expected to find on their dinner plate at a frat house and suspected that the last-minute cancellations and very late arrivals of some invitees were more about dreading tuna noodle casserole than scheduling conflicts. This year, one of the founders of Pyramid Breweries was on the guest list and I planned a menu to complement the company's range of beers. But when my food delivery had not arrived by 11:00 A.M. that Monday, I locked myself in the kitchen, posting a note on the door:

DON'T COME IN UNLESS YOU MUST.
MY DELIVERY IS NOT HERE.
I HAVE NOTHING FOR DINNER.
I AM HAVING A MELTDOWN.

But Richard, who'd gone from pledge class leader to house manager to vice president in less than two years, defied the note and opened the kitchen door, confronting my tears with a smile. "What do you have?" he asked me calmly and opened my nearly bare fridges to reveal lemons, habanero peppers, and celery. And when he turned to me still smiling confidently and told me that I could surely do something with that, I knew he wasn't really expecting a celery salad with lemon habanero vinaigrette; I knew that what he was really saying was that it was going to be okay, that it was, after all, just dinner. And right at that moment, junior Steven arrived holding cases of various Pyramid beers in his arms, announcing that at least he'd secured the one essential ingredient for any frat event. John tracked down the truck and brought me some of what I needed immediately and when my driver did finally arrive with the rest, he took one look at the haggard, grease-soaked wench before him and told me that he could see how much love and passion I had for my guys. And the meal that President Nick assured me we could just cancel, no problem, went forward, including a beer cheese that I had researched and then adapted to be something uniquely local, proudly presenting it to our guest, who made fun of the very idea. But the guys thought that putting beer into cheese was inspired.

It wasn't long after the Pyramid dinner that recently graduated Newman returned as our guest and I once again set out to impress, this time more sure of the reception. I decided to make a vanilla cake to accompany some fresh strawberries, but once the cakes were made, I realized they weren't going to feed all eighty guys and so I further complicated my life by making homemade vanilla custard and whipped cream to create a sort of trifle. And then I realized I needed to make a quick jam, too. And of course I couldn't just make more goddamn cake because I'd spent twenty minutes stirring custard to make a trifle. You start out with a simple idea and before you know it, you're on your way to Monday night dinner hell.

And it only got worse when one of the freshmen brought flowers and as I was cutting the stems, snipped so severely into my index finger that I wasn't entirely sure how much finger I had left. But it was one of the major events of the year and there was just no question of stopping. I wrapped the wound and pulled three pairs of gloves over it as several pledges watched in horror and because I didn't immediately seek medical attention, the wound required surgery several days later, which was not in retrospect the greatest example of good judgment. But by god, they could see I was a hard worker and that was my real intent.

A few days earlier, I had opened the compost bin to find stacks of notebooks and pens dumped thoughtlessly on top of the food scraps and just as Johnny, one of the live-outs, was driving into the parking lot, he saw me hurling the books into the air like I'd lost my mind. "Are you okay?" he asked as he watched me storm back toward the House and I turned to reply rhetorically, "Who does that?" I received an answer seconds later when he called out "Charlie," having collected the offending material with its owner identified. Johnny had caught a freshman sticking his fork back into a communal bowl of pineapple the day before and had had a similar reaction to mine, at first challenging the offender and then rolling his eyes and shaking his head, defeated. It was the cumulative tiny acts of laziness and boneheadedness that made you insane enough to want to demonstrate that a little thing like a finger gushing blood was not going to stop you from doing your job.

And then something would happen to make you forget all of the frustration and restore the love. Just days before spring break, Hanley, a sophomore who'd had to move back home out of state, appeared in the kitchen with his pledge brother Riley. "Can you get this guy some scrambled eggs?" Riley had asked. And I turned to see his arm around Hanley, who was smiling broadly. I had barely known this returning brother who almost never spoke to me when he lived in the House, and had assumed he was like a number of the guys indifferent to my efforts. But when I handed him a plate, he said, "It's good having your food again." And it reminded me that we don't always know the impact we have on other people until later, if we ever know, a lesson I would get frequently from these guys.

FOR THE FOURTH YEAR in a row, my husband and I chose a spring break destination where we were fairly certain no one would have any idea what it means to cook in a fraternity, but where we knew the food would be great and I would find inspiration. This time it was Istanbul, a very modern Muslim country that seemed just enough out of our comfort zone while still allowing us sinful pleasures like free will and a bottle of wine with dinner.

It was all going so well, the sky bright blue and the sun shining, when we took a boat to a coastal village on our last day and we sat on a bench for the journey with dozens of other passengers, our feet propped up against the railings. And then on my right side, a young man asked me where I was from and began to tell me about his own life failures and his hatred of the West so calmly that an observer would never have known how chilling it was, how it actually crossed my mind that these might be my last moments on earth. And I thought to myself that of all the people on this planet allowed to be miserable and angry at that moment, he and I, on our way to an island retreat on a perfect day, were not two of them. And then suddenly we were at our destination and the man disappeared into a crowd, leaving my husband and me to sit at a restaurant on the edge of the Bosporus eating fried mussels and just-caught bass with a thick garlic sauce and looking out at the sunlight dancing on the water and wishing life could always be like this.

We arrived home late on Sunday, with no time to buy groceries for the next morning, let alone catch up with the news, so I was unaware that something really terrible had happened that last day of spring break—just not to me. I reluctantly dragged myself out of bed the next morning, checking my phone as I did every workday for an indication of what I might be facing. The first text that morning was from Richard, but it wasn't like any text before:

Riley McCarthy passed away this afternoon. The brotherhood just found out. Please be supportive.

And what kept going through my head as I drove into work were those last three words, as if he needed to say them. Maybe it was just the stress of the news, a plea rather than an indictment. But I couldn't help wondering if the progress I'd made in the past couple of years was more about me than them.

12

Many Hungers

On the Sunday that I flew back from Istanbul a new group of spring pledges moved into the House, strangers to everyone but a handful of the guys already there. That same day the TV was on with no one in particular watching, reporting that several young men had been caught in an avalanche while snowboarding at Steven's Pass—their fate and identities unclear. Slowly they began to pay attention to the news and word spread among the guys that Riley had been there, that he'd hit a tree and been buried in snow, that Stuart, another Alpha Sig, had been with him and had managed to dig his friend out and had tried to breathe life back. It was late in the evening at the House and there'd been a lot of drinking on this last day of spring break, but suddenly the party was over.

When I walked into my kitchen Monday morning, one of the pledges was in the dish room carrying out tasks like someone who wasn't sure what he was doing, and I sympathized with these new recruits who'd walked into a dark story they weren't part of. The first familiar face was Richard's, red-eyed and lips quivering as he reached for a hug. He'd quickly established himself as a leader and had on numerous occasions had to officially punish or fine or otherwise chastise Riley, which he always did in that loving "really, Riley, *again?*" exasperated sort of way.

And then one of the guys who'd recently moved out openly sobbed as he greeted me with, "I am so glad to see you. I am so glad to see you *here.*" Blair had just returned from his study abroad in Ecuador, and having missed out on the last months of Riley's life, he recalled the last time they'd spoken, the last meaningless encounter, now huge in significance. And then others gathered in the kitchen to do the same, laughing about their first impressions of him in their pledge class, standing out from the clean-cut crowd as they all wondered, "Who in the hell is this guy?" We talked about the Dick's Drive-In incident and the morning he had so enraged me with his antics that I'd walked off the job. When I pulled out the apology letter he'd written, one of his pledge brothers, Martel, asked to see it. He held it gently and when he was finished reading, he handed it back to me remarking that "it hurts to see it, but it makes it seem like he's still here."

Dear Darlene,
I am sorry for the comments I made on Friday morning.
My actions were not made in anger or in hate towards you;
they were just stupid drunk jokes. I understand that I was
being very disrespectful and I am very sorry. That type of
disrespect does not belong in this house, especially towards
you. I hope there are no hard feelings.
Sincerely,
Riley McCarthy

Four days into that heavy week, Devin asked me to participate in the viral national practical joke and brilliant marketing scheme of placing a bottle of Smirnoff Ice in an unexpected location and tricking someone into discovering it, at which point the victim was required to drink the whole bottle in one attempt on bended knee. The term for it was "Iced" and Devin's target was Steven. "I'm just going to put it in the fridge by the potato salad and when he comes in, you just need to ask him to get the salad for you." Any other week I might have refused to be a party to something like that, but it was not just any week. And when Steven walked right into the trap, I was laughing as hard as anyone as he turned to Johnny, who held a camera phone ready to record the whole thing. "Our cook just Iced me," Steven exclaimed in disbelief, but hours later, when he returned to the kitchen to ask for a gallon of milk, it was my turn to discover his trap. At first I flatly refused to get on my knees and knock back a bottle of booze in the middle of the workday, but Steven followed me as I put out lunch, wailing at the unfairness, and so I relented. It took me a painfully long time and attracted several of the guys into the kitchen as spectators, and that, too, was captured on film, broadcast on Facebook with the caption, SWEET REVENGE. Two days later, at Riley's funeral, I leaned over to Bob to ask who had been Riley's fraternity big brother, knowing that whomever it was would be especially hurting now, especially in need of the slack I was pretty stingy in giving. "Steven," he whispered.

Riley had not been one of the kitchen chat regulars; in a house that big you couldn't be close to everyone and I let each of them decide how much they wanted to interact. But I was amazed when I tried to recall the times I'd engaged with him and realized there were very many such little moments: the time he saw Blair rolling balls of chopped garlic and thought they were coconut cookies and still wanted to bite into one when we enlightened him; the time I made fun of his lettuce cravings by packing a gallon container with green leaves and labeling it RILEY'S MIDNIGHT SNACK, to which he added the line HANDS OFF! lest anyone think to take it from him; the time he'd eaten six skewers of Vietnamese grilled pork with peanut sauce, exposing the lie that he ate nothing but lettuce sandwiches and cereal. There were so many seemingly meaningless memories like that, things I'd barely noticed at the time, a reminder of how benignly careless I could be with the people around me, not giving them my full attention, often just hearing without listening.

I had known very well that he was the House clown, but it wasn't until his vigil that I learned of the more three-dimensional person from the stories the guys told: that he'd just decided to major in engineering, that he read other people's textbooks for fun because they "looked interesting." Casey talked about being despondent over an exam recently when Riley's goofiness had lifted him. And one of his childhood friends remembered his generosity, often sharing Ritz crackers with the ragtag bunch of hungry kids he hung out with while BMX biking. Stuart, who'd been with Riley at the end, looked like he hadn't slept or shaved in some time, and was stung by the attacks on their decision to snowboard that day, and spoke of how happy he'd been right to the last moments of life. And when Riley's cousin Jessi gave the eulogy, telling a story about his grandparents' raspberry patch, I realized he was much closer to my heart than I'd known:

*Riley was over there every day during growing season.
In fact, if Granny wanted any berries for herself at all,
she had to be up and outside well before Riley. The
raspberries were just the beginning of his unique eating
habits and a prelude to the large portions he would
consume later in life. One of our favorite family stories
has to do with Granny's homemade jam. About ten
years ago Granny began rationing her jam. At Christmas
each family received one jar, except the McCarthy
family always got four jars or more. I never really
understood the equity of this distribution system.
Turns out Riley loved homemade jam. He could easily
consume a jar in one sitting. His brother Mike
described his consumption as one part toast or biscuit,
two parts jam. Riley's love continued into his adult
life. In fact, Mike visited the fraternity earlier this week
and discovered a jar in Riley's closet, about three-
quarters of the way gone. Apparently Riley was hoard-
ing Granny's jam.*

And it was at that moment that another small memory
surfaced and I whispered, "oh my god, the jam!" to my husband, who was seated next to me. I had spent the previous
summer canning fruit and brought jars of blueberry jam to
the House in the fall, unable to find a commercial product
through our food supplier that was just fruit and real sugar. I
knew that this was one of my obsessions and that the guys
were probably, depressingly, just as happy opening those little
plastic packs of Kraft jelly. But one day in October, as I was
putting something in the guys' fridge, I heard a wistful voice

behind me. "I think I might eat this whole jar. I love it so much." And I turned to see Riley holding a spoon and a near-empty Mason jar, in total rapt concentration on something that I sensed was not really about my homemade blueberry jam, but about something much bigger. I played the memory over and over in my head and searched my brain for other food moments and remembered the cake I'd made out of the blue the previous October, with the icing that wasn't like "normal" icing, something I rarely ever did, and realized suddenly that it was his twentieth and last birthday cake. But of course we didn't know.

Weeks into the quarter, Blair, who had returned to helping me in the kitchen, told me that he had been having a normal sort of day when he thought about Riley and had felt stricken and cried uncontrollably. "Is that normal?" he asked me, really obviously wondering if *he* was normal. And I thought about the weeks after my father's death, when I was not much older than these guys, and how I had stood in a bookstore in New Orleans suddenly frozen in grief and wondered why anyone reads anything because nothing matters. I was twenty-seven when he died and it had not gotten better over the years the way they said it would; you went on, and you laughed and were happy about other things, but it was never going to be okay that he wasn't there. "Totally normal," I assured him.

LOVE YOU DARLENE. YOUR SECRET ADMIRER greeted me on the whiteboard of my kitchen door a few days after the funeral, a welcome reminder of what kept me in that job year after year. In other handwriting, someone had written YOUR OTHER SECRET ADMIRER. I was pretty sure that these were from my sorority groupies, but when YOUR ALUMNI SECRET ADMIRER appeared, I figured it was one of the guys who'd attended a meeting at the House the night before. For several more days, there were additions that brightened an otherwise bleak time, until SOME CREEPY GUY appeared, which made me smile, too, but I decided it was time to erase the thread before it degenerated any further.

The rest of that year was subdued, the usual levity of spring quarter weighted by the absence of someone who defined fun, but there were still welcome and needed moments of comic relief that season. It had been years since the House was plagued with rodents, so that spring when I discovered teeth marks on wholesale-size bars of chocolate and open maple syrup jars in my pantry, I suspected a rat called Alpha Sig. I couldn't picture a two-pound critter lifting a ten-pound chocolate bar, even if he could balance himself between the bags of polenta and boxes of brown sugar, let alone having the dexterity to remove jar lids. It was more likely that a chimpanzee had escaped from Woodland Park Zoo, which we'd have heard about, so the source had to be one of the guys in the House. But Blair was indignant and conducted experiments to prove me wrong, which is exactly what you expect of a college student. "See!" he declared in triumph as he showed me a section he'd bitten and compared it to the suspect portion. "Definitely not human!" He couldn't explain the maple syrup vandalism, but I made a note to ask Larry the pest control guy about it.

Blair was in the kitchen when Larry made his routine visit, hair slicked back and appearing in his usual one-size-too-tight uniform buttoned up to his neck and pants a good two inches too short, asking with a creepy sort of excitement, "What can I do for you today?" Before I could answer, he peered over at the halibut I was preparing and started offering unsolicited advice, which irritated the hell out of me. For some reason, it never bothered me when the firemen would stop into the kitchen and swap recipes and tips with me, but it got under my skin to have the exterminator giving me cooking lessons. We'd had different reps over the years and most of them were perfectly normal people who could just as easily have been checking the water meter as the mousetraps, but Larry was the sort of person you'd suspect had bodies hidden in his backyard. It didn't help that Blair instantly recognized him as the guy he'd seen a few weeks back wandering suspiciously around the House, probably just doing his job, but in a way that made him want to call the cops. The whole halibut thing made me forget about the chocolate and when he'd gone, I asked, "Who aspires to that job?" I figured Blair was at the age when huge lifestyle choices are made. And then I thought how the path isn't always clear, how I'd majored in English and somehow missed the fork in the road that led to food editor at *Bon Appétit* instead of frat house hash slinger. I figured it was probably the same for the health inspector, the least welcome person in the neighborhood.

Because I had decided to leave at the end of the year, I treated my last health inspection with the sort of wildly sarcastic attitude I had only fantasized about before, ignoring the adage about burning bridges. It wasn't that I rejected basic principles of food safety; it was that I'd become convinced over the years that if you cooked in a frat house, they were going to find something wrong no matter how diligent you were about cooking ground beef to 155 degrees and keeping your raw chicken separate from the deli meats. They seemed to have a quota of penalty points, so that if you left pasta salad unrefrigerated or had duck breasts hanging in the basement to dry into prosciutto, they were done with you quickly. But if they couldn't find any of the usual violations, they'd ask to see your bathrooms (a mortifying request even when it came from the food delivery guy desperate for a break), or they'd tell you the Dumpsters were overflowing or that your mouse-traps were pointed the wrong way. It was always something. The year before, the inspector had insisted I post a hand-washing diagram by the sink, which I dutifully did, adding my own notation after he left that the guys were not to "re-move or deface this stupid sign." So instead they hung it upside down. At what was to be my final inspection, he handed me a stack of cartoon drawings of safe food practices with expla-nations written at a second-grade reading level. I thought it odd because the department had just gone through a paperless overhaul, equipping the inspectors with new laptops only to have them suddenly handing out dubiously educational color-ing books.

Final health inspection done, major formal dinners over with, and spring pledges initiated, the year was drawing to a close, but unlike other colleges around the country, there were still two weeks of school left after the Memorial Day week-end. My husband and I spent the holiday as we often did at the Folklife Festival, the outdoor music event at the Seattle Center that marks the beginning of summer, with Bumbershoot closing it out on Labor Day weekend. I was there on Saturday sitting in the grass and enjoying the sun, but I was annoyed by the high concentration that year of what I called "brain-pickled trolls," the aging hippies waving colored scarves that drew attention to themselves and obscured the view of the bands we were there to see, when I received a voice mail from Blair.

"I'm with Corey and Gene and we were looking at our dinner options and saw Kraft mac and cheese, your favorite, and we were wondering if we could come to your house for dinner." I texted him, asking if they were high and letting him know we were having soft shell crabs *for two.* "Okay, well then just me and Corey," he replied. And I let him know that the two were my husband and I. The next day as I set lunch out, Corey, who would soon be leaving for law school in San Francisco, told me that they weren't just drunk calling, that "we really were hungry, but thought there was less than a fifty percent chance you'd say yes." And it was like someone holding up a great big mirror when you are looking your very worst.

Blair told me they weren't the only ones starving over the long weekend, that Bernie had taken bread out of the freezer they were expressly forbidden to touch, the same freezer I'd placed various signs on over the years, aiming for clarity: THIS IS MY FREEZER, NOT YOUR BEER FRIDGE, DO NOT ADD OR RE-MOVE ITEMS, I RELY ON THE CONTENTS TO PREPARE YOUR MEALS, and finally the straight-to-the-point KEEP OUT. And just to stir things up, he confronted the culprit about it in my presence that Tuesday. "I told Darlene about your weekend bread-stealing," he taunted Bernie, who stammered that "Riley McCarthy taught me to do that." And suddenly we were all three very quiet and I thought about Riley resourcefully finding a way to transport jam to his mouth and teaching his younger brother where to find the bread, the way my older son, Sean, had taught baby Simon to open all the Christmas presents days before the holiday one year.

Not half an hour later, Blair returned from the freezer with a note he found taped to it:

I WILL NOT TAKE ANY MORE BREAD.
SORRY FOR THE ENCONVINENCE.
ANYONOMOUS

And in the top left corner of the page were several failed attempts at the correct execution of "inconvenience," which he never did get right, but no similar efforts over the thoroughly unconvincing "anonymous." And we laughed as we recalled the time that a flustered Bernie had posted a signed note on the front door misspelling his own name. I loved these twelve words, not just because of what they said about the incident in question, but for all the other messages within them about respect and concern for what I thought of the writer. I would think back to this fondly when several weeks later Blair shared phone-video footage of Brian from a party the night before, acting like an ass as he pulled chili and bacon out of the freezer and waved it over his head in a sort of Darlene-defying dance.

A couple of weeks after the year ended, Corey, Carlos, Shane, Blair, and Richard came to my home for dinner. My husband photographed the six of us standing with our arms around each other, all smiles. They'd been thrilled at the invitation, not the way your adult friends are when you invite them over and they have to check their crammed calendars and give you a list of the foods they can't or won't eat and you start to wish you'd never asked. I made Bacon and Caramelized Onion Tart, Home-Cured Salmon, Paella, and tiny sugar snap peas, followed by Strawberry-Rhubarb Crisp, the sort of menu that was impractical for seventy-five guys. I'd made a special trip to the Spanish Table to buy a paella pan large enough for this gathering and bought a folding table from

Ikea because the usual dining table in our condo was too small. And we took them on our roof with its view of the Space Needle and Mt. Rainier. I promised to have more of these dinners over the summer with other invitees, but that was the only one, my own crammed calendar getting in the way. And anyway, I had quit my job, a regular act my husband, Phil, had ceased to comment on, understanding why I would want to and at the same time *not* want to.

Later that month, when the loss of purpose and a clear sense of future goals were hitting me particularly hard, I was reading Amy Sedaris's wickedly funny *I Like You*, helpfully subtitled *Hospitality Under the Influence*. When I came across her gift idea of a Fuck It Bucket, it struck me as equally appropriate for both the college graduate and someone diagnosed with a terminal illness, filled as she instructed with treats and a card suggesting that when faced with a particularly bad patch, the recipient just give in and have a piece of candy. I loved this idea so much that I immediately went to Target to buy candy, thinking I would bring it over to the house for Corey, who was about to leave for law school, where he would no doubt find many occasions to reach for the bucket. But when I got to the aisles of sodium benzoate–laced, high fructose corn syrup, red dye number 5 treats, I just couldn't do it, despite the fact that I'd been known to say "fuck it, I'll have another cocktail" more than once in my life, which was arguably at least as bad as anything on the candy aisle. But I couldn't help it; I cared so much about their well-being that compromise was not even possible for me anymore.

Two days later, Richard sent me a text: "You are missed. We are drunk. Hobo Party." And attached was a photograph of one of the guys with a cardboard sign around his neck declaring WILL WORK 4 DARLENE'S FOOD, an effective use of technology to remind me that while I believed I had moved on from a life resembling one constant frat party, they were not letting go so easily. But the subtle begging was hardly necessary. I had thought early on that they needed me, but I'd learned over time that it was really the other way around. I didn't need the paycheck, but I had to work, and not just so that my days would have structure. It wasn't just autonomy and control that I got from working there; it was the knowledge that no matter how awful I could be and how wrong, these guys always had my back, as if I were one of their kind.

When Adam Thompson of the *Wall Street Journal* asked me to name some of the more elaborate dishes I prepared for the guys, I went blank, thinking only of the basic but real food I make with fresh ingredients. The following are some of the dishes most frequently requested.

Creamy Penne with Chicken and Smoked Sausage

FOR ABOUT 20 PEOPLE (2 13x9-INCH CASSEROLE DISHES):

2 lbs. penne pasta
5 lbs. chicken, breast or thigh or a combination, cut
    into strips
Cajun seasoning (recipe follows)
1 T. plus 1½ tsp. coarse salt, divided
1 lb. andouille or other smoked sausage, cubed
4 oz. butter
1 cup flour
2 T. dry mustard
7 cups whole milk
4½ cups heavy cream
1½ tsp. pepper
2½ lbs. cheese blend (a mixture of mozzarella, provo-
    lone, Parmesan)
4 oz. Parmesan

Cook the pasta until not quite tender, toss with olive oil to prevent sticking, and set aside. Toss the chicken with some

Cajun seasoning and the tablespoon of salt and grill or sauté until almost cooked through. Set aside. Sauté the sausage until some of the fat is rendered and it browns. Set aside. Melt the butter, stir in the flour and mustard, and cook 1 or 2 minutes. Slowly add the milk and cream and bring to a boil. Reduce to a simmer until thickened. Season with the 1½ teaspoons salt, pepper, and additional Cajun seasoning to taste. Stir in the pasta and pour into 2 13x9-inch pans. Top with cheese blend and additional Parmesan. Bake at 350 degrees until hot and lightly browned.

Cajun Seasoning

There is no salt in the mix intentionally. This allows you to add more or less spice without affecting the salt level, which you should adjust separately. You can buy commercial Cajun seasoning mixes, but they generally have far fewer spices than this homemade version:

2 T. onion powder
2 T. granulated garlic
2 T. dried oregano
2 T. dried basil
1 T. dried thyme leaves
2 T. freshly ground black pepper
1 T. cayenne pepper
1 T. celery seed
2½ T. smoked paprika
2½ T. sweet paprika

Combine all of the ingredients and store in a jar.

Marinara Sauce

I'm not opposed to some prepared ingredients. I wasn't
generally making my own mayonnaise and ketchup, or even
my own bread for that matter, but I could never understand
canned spaghetti sauce. It's one of the easiest things to make
from scratch and the way it makes the kitchen smell for hours
is reward enough. Makes about a gallon and freezes well.

2 small or 1 medium onion, chopped
12 garlic cloves, chopped
¼ cup olive oil
¼ cup tomato paste
1 T red pepper flakes
1 cup white wine
2 28-oz. cans crushed organic tomatoes
2 28-oz. cans diced organic tomatoes
2 T dried oregano
1½ T black pepper
2 bay leaves
1 cup fresh basil leaves, chopped

Sauté onions and garlic in the olive oil. Add tomato paste
and cook for a couple of minutes until the paste darkens
slightly. Add the remaining ingredients, except for the basil,
and simmer for an hour or so, or until desired consistency.
Remove the bay leaves and stir in the basil.

Chicken and Sausage Jambalaya

7 lbs. boneless, skinless chicken thigh meat, cubed
3 lbs. smoked sausage, diced
½ cup vegetable oil
Cajun seasoning (recipe above)
4 stalks celery, diced
1 large green bell pepper, diced
2 onions, chopped
30 garlic cloves, chopped
8 oz. tomato paste
2 T. Tabasco
1 T. salt
3 lbs. (7 cups) raw white rice
12 cups chicken stock
1 bunch green onions, chopped
1 cup chopped parsley

Sauté the chicken and sausage in the oil, seasoning to taste. Add the celery, bell pepper, onion, and garlic and continue to sauté until softened. Add the tomato paste, Tabasco, and salt. Stir in the rice and chicken stock and cover. Bake at 350 degrees for 45 minutes to an hour, or until the chicken is cooked through and the rice has absorbed the liquid and is tender. Stir in the green onions and parsley.

13

Insider

Don't let anyone die and don't let Darlene quit.
—PARTING WORDS OF ADVICE FROM OUTGOING FRATERNITY
PRESIDENT KEV TO INCOMING PRESIDENT GAVIN

When Gavin told me about that exchange with Kev, we both laughed, but there was also a tinge of sadness to it. Riley had died during Kev's tenure and although it had been an accident far removed from the House, the responsibility of leading the brotherhood through those days had been a heavy one. Everything else could be a catastrophe, but the continuity in the kitchen and the predictability of a fresh hot meal was something that kept everyone together. Anyone could do the job, but as Bob once told Badley during his presidency when Badley had grown just a little weary of me, "It takes a special sort of woman to *want* to do this job."

At the end of each school year, my food sales guy John would tell his boss, Rod, that the Alpha Sig account was in jeopardy because "Darlene's not coming back next year." And every year Rod, who'd been around from the start, would sigh and smile, "Yes she is. She loves those guys." It annoyed the hell out of me because every time I said that I was leaving I really, really meant it! By my fifth year, Rod had been promoted twice and was director of sales, someone with the power to make changes, so I was glad that he was still taking my whiny calls. But I'd had enough by the end of that year and when he visited the House, I said it all again. "It's dirty work. It's exhausting. It doesn't pay enough. I don't need to do this." And just as the words were out of my mouth, one of the guys ran down the stairs and out the back door yelling, "Bye, Darlene, love you, Darlene!" And there was nothing more to say.

In mid-July, after I'd agreed to return for a sixth year, I was in New York City on a getaway with my mom for her birthday, and I was having trouble sleeping, tormented by doubts about the decision. I was close to backing out and as we walked across the Brooklyn Bridge, there was a chalk-written note at my feet: JUST DEAL WITH IT. The next day, near our hotel was a similar sentiment, although somewhat more reassuring: IT'S GOING TO BE FINE . . . BREATHE. And if I hadn't known better, I'd have thought Richard was behind it; it was the kind of thing I might expect to see written near the Alpha Sig kitchen front door on any given Monday morning.

A couple of weeks before my trip, he'd come to my house with Bob for brunch to see what help I might be in finding and training a replacement. In his hands were papers that appeared to be salary data and Bob held out a book he wanted me to read, Michael Kimmel's *Guyland*, subtitled *The Perilous World Where Boys Become Men, Understanding the Crit-*

ical Years Between 16 and 26. I knew nothing about the book, but there was only one reason for me to read something with a title like that. It was as if they were saying, "We know we make you crazy, but please don't leave us." Richard understood that he was the one person most likely to change my mind, but what he didn't tell me was that he'd be studying in Belgium for more than half the upcoming year. "I didn't tell you," he later confessed, "because I was afraid you wouldn't come back if you knew."

There were things that hadn't changed from my first day on the job. I knew this immediately when I saw juniors Martel and Watson proudly fixing a hole in the wall outside my kitchen on the first day of Work Week. They were expecting a prize until I pointed out that at my own house there's never been a baseball-size hole to begin with. I still had to put up necessarily repetitive signs before a holiday like:

ANY FOOD LEFT IN THE FRIDGE BY FRIDAY
SHOULD BE THROWN OUT.
DO NOT EAT AFTER FRIDAY.
FOOD EATEN NEXT WEEK MAY KILL YOU.

And despite my vow to be a more civil customer, it was just weeks into the school year when a delivery screw-up had me firing off the kind of email to multiple recipients that leaves you feeling almost as bad the next morning as if you'd slept with your sister's husband. Blair could sense that I was especially low and I told him about the incident and the email. "I'm almost afraid to read what I wrote. I was pretty drunk at the time," I confessed as I pulled out my computer. But instead of adding to my self-flagellation, he roared with laughter, no doubt having been there himself. And I smiled as I looked up at him, knowing that no matter how judged and beaten down I sometimes felt in the outside world, there was always someone here on my side.

And it wasn't just Blair; it was all of them as a team. I was feeling particularly ready to bolt one night that December when I noticed a car parked behind mine, blocking my exit, a vehicle whose owner appeared to be unknown. So I texted my husband that it might be a rather long time before I escaped. I exercised all the adult problem-solving skills you expect of someone in that situation, with thoughts of a tow truck or, failing that, a ride home and a bus trip the next day, all of it such a hassle.

But a few of the guys, seeing me standing there helpless and annoyed, and upon establishing that the owner of the offending vehicle was not anyone they knew, did the obvious; they marshaled every available brother in the House and marched past me on a mission, intending to physically lift the trespasser to a place most likely to cause immediate law enforcement attention. "No one fucks with our chef!" they called out to the owner, who was suddenly running toward the Alpha Sig House, completely frantic at the sight of his car in the air, held up by little more than righteous indignation. And while I did not ask for this or encourage it, and could see a hundred ways for it to go very badly, and thought it frattish in the extreme, I totally loved them for it; it was just one more of the ways they'd always been there.

Still, a lot had changed. There were many more engineering than business or liberal arts majors in the freshmen class, a reflection of tighter standards for admission and an economy offering little to people without a science degree. And I had the ease and confidence of someone who owned the place, all the fear of heavy testosterone exposure long gone. It had been daunting that first year to walk into a house full of strange young men, but I'd seen enough to know that what was on the surface was only a tiny part of the story.

But what most changed was the food; after years of being told I was crazy and difficult and deluded, I was finally getting my way. "Your name came up at our last all-company sales meeting," John told me weeks into the new year. He said a speaker had been presenting a new line of deli meats and he'd paused as he yelled, "Where's Sutey, John Sutey from Seattle?" A sea of heads turned to him as he raised his hand. "This should please your customer who cares about this sort of thing," he said before describing humanely raised and antibiotic-free animals—like this was some kind of new invention. "We were all talking about you at our last meeting," my former sales guy Kirk told me shortly after this, assuring me that they didn't talk about everyone. But I knew that the second-largest food distributor in the nation wasn't rolling out new products just for me; other voices, bigger and more important ones, were being heard. When the pink slime story broke later that year and suddenly the whole country seemed awakened to the question I'd asked their meat buyer years ago—"what's in my ground beef?"—it was with no small amount of sweet satisfaction that I beat John over the head with the "I told you so"s.

But I'd long since stopped waiting for the big guys to take me seriously, and the August before I returned to work I found a small company supplying all the local meat, poultry, and fish I could ask for. I'd spent weeks trying to contact them, hearing nothing in response to several emails. Finally I sent a message that while I knew they supplied the best restaurants in Seattle and that we were just a frat house, I'd spent close to a hundred thousand dollars on meat the previous year. In short order I was sitting across from two sales reps in the Solarium, listening to their pitch before I had to stop them. "I'm sorry," I said. "You just don't understand how freakish it is to be talked to like I'm not a crazy person."

So my first lunch was Carlton Farms Pork Cheek and Black-Eyed Pea Chili. And that year was filled with things like chicken garlic sausage from Uli's in Pike Place Market and brisket from Northwest Grass-Fed Beef. But new products meant new challenges, as I learned when the sixty pounds of lamb shoulder I ordered yielded only thirty when the trimming was done.

I had written LAMB TAGINE on the posted menu, but I knew I didn't have enough yield for a stew and would need to turn this into a kind of Greek lamb pasta dish. And I was thinking about this when junior Kev walked into the kitchen. He was the president at the time, but in prior years had been one of those I'd described as so afraid of me he'd put water on his cereal before he'd ask me for milk. It wasn't until his leadership role made him partly responsible for keeping me around that he discovered I didn't bite. And he'd immediately become one of my favorites when he'd said that he was "pretty certain any good idea out of Blair's mouth originated in Darlene's brain," which Blair found less funny than I did. He'd read the menu and came into the kitchen to ask, "What's a tagine?" And I looked up at him still thinking about how to recover. "Never mind. You're not having that," I declared. "You're having 'Darlene Fucked Up the Meat Order Pasta.'" It was something I could never have said to the Robertsons, but Kev just smiled warmly. "Sounds delicious," he said in a way that made it clear that he could think of nothing better for dinner, that he didn't even want tagine, whatever that was, and that tagine was old news.

My stridency on food matters had only increased over the years, but I had mellowed considerably in my dealings with the guys from the days when I was known to actually throw things. On what would have been Riley's twenty-first birthday, Blair pulled off his shirt to reveal a tattoo—Riley's name in the shape of omega and the date of his accident—that nearly covered his right shoulder. Richard had warned me that Blair had a surprise for me, and a lot of thoughts went through my mind when I saw that he had literally fired a memory into his skin. He had been completely sober when he'd done it, but I think my reaction would have been the same.

"I knew you'd react like that," Richard told me later. And when I asked what he meant, that I hadn't said a thing, he clarified. "That's what I mean. I knew you wouldn't judge." I might still have such strong opinions that I was hard to be around sometimes, but some of these guys had become my family and the love was unconditional. That is why, when a severe ice storm screamed into Seattle that winter that had Bob sending me National Weather Service reports that it was far too dangerous for me to go into work, I pulled on snow boots and headed down the hill, knowing I'd have to walk half the distance where the bus drivers couldn't go. "Only essential services are operating at UW," my husband had assured me. And I looked at him like someone who has a normal job and doesn't really understand. "I *am* an essential service."

When Delta Gamma's annual Anchor Splash fund-raiser approached, I had further confirmation that the guys themselves were leading the drive for fresh food. That year's Alpha

Sig representative appeared in my kitchen with armloads of groceries he'd bought and wanted me to prepare for him, the usual colorful but monotonous diet of grilled chicken, asparagus, and sweet potatoes that I'd first learned about from Newman. I was in a tense mood that day, not helped by a health inspection just minutes before Michael stood beaming, his smile slowly fading as I explained that I had no time for this. But when he said "no worries," and began to walk away, I relented on the condition that I would be teaching and not doing. And as he pulled out his ingredients, I noticed that the packaging on the chicken was Draper Farms. "And organic, too," he grinned. "All of it, the vegetables, too." And not that there's any real meaning at all, but that year, for the first time, Alpha Sigs placed a respectable third.

Our Fourth Annual Pig Roast that year was overseen by junior Watson, who had built his own pizza oven and who often shared stories with me about helping in his grandfather's garden and catching and smoking his own fish. Even Newman, the founder of this tradition, had not approached it with such pride. There had been years when I had come in to work and found that not only was the roast not under way, or the coals lit, but the pig was not even in the House. However, when I arrived that year, Watson was sitting on the porch nursing a beer at 7:00 A.M. as an already-bronzing animal was spinning over the coals. And unlike some in the past who grew bored with the whole thing by noon, turning it over to pledges, Watson was there to the end, taking breaks for work and class, but otherwise watching over his baby.

I was in the kitchen when I heard a familiar song blaring over the speakers they had placed outside. I stopped everything and walked toward the patio, where l leaned against the back door and listened to Big IZ singing "Over the Rainbow," the same song Newman had chosen to end Kevin's vigil. None of the guys standing around drinking and laughing and tending the coals had known the person whose happy photographs still remained like a shrine in a corner of the House, but as I stood there listening to that song so full of memories for me, I could see that a thread of tradition ran through the years that tied them all together.

And that year saw the return of several alumni I'd watched come and go, including Matt, who'd left the fraternity in his second year, explaining to me that he felt he didn't fit in and reminding me of all the times in my life I'd felt the same. He had later moved back into the House, finding a welcome that surprised him and he'd stayed until he'd graduated and married. "I'm the guest speaker!" he told me when he startled me at the back door. And he had come back not just to inspire a whole new crowd, but also stayed on to tutor a few of them in math, something he'd been doing for a while, I learned, and I couldn't help thinking of the irony.

Not long afterward, Eliab, who'd been the "black dude for fraternity president" who had inspired Carlos to join, stopped in to pick something up, regretting that he couldn't stay to eat. He asked me how the new pledges were treating me and I told him that it was a different world. "They're well-mannered and smart and spend all their time in the library," I told him before sighing that "I sort of miss the old days with you clowns." And he laughed as he looked at the brisket and scalloped potatoes waiting to go out and said, "That's what I miss."

It was Badley, though, who had remained a periodic presence in my life and not just a rare visitor. At the start of the year, I'd received a call from the HR department of a top company in DC conducting a background check on him. The caller had asked a lot of questions I had trouble answering despite my claim that Badley was especially dear to me, which made me feel stupid and rather useless as a reference. And I said I didn't know exactly what he'd done after working for Senator Murray other than bussing tables at his new employer's elite parties, just like I wasn't sure what his hobbies were, besides texting me. But in the end it didn't matter what I said and he got the job. Badley, whom I had sometimes found incoherent as a freshman, truly had his shit together now.

It was two years after he graduated and moved out that I received an email from him asking for my best ratatouille recipe, as if I had several in my arsenal. "It's vegetarian, right?" he added, tipping me off that this was for Monica, the same girl he'd been trying to impress with his nonbacon cookies at his internship just out of school. "I need it by 1:45 your time," he concluded, giving me the three busiest hours during my day to respond. And rather than send a rigid recipe, I sent him the basic concept, which I thought was simple enough and allowed flexibility in ingredients. What I got back was the following:

I have a few questions regarding your recipe. Please see them below.
Eggplant (How many?)
Zucchini (How many?)
Yellow squash (How many?)
Red bell pepper (How many?)
Olive oil (How much?)

Preheat oven to 400 degrees (do I preheat before I start cutting veggies?). **Cut these vegetables into chunks and**

toss in olive oil (how much oil? Do I toss it in a bowl or in a frying pan/iron skillet on the stove?). **Season with a little salt and pepper** (How much?). **Roast for around 15 minutes or until tender and slightly browned** (what kind of pans will I need for this?). **The eggplant will probably take longer (make sure it's all the way cooked through and tender)** (how can I tell when eggplant is cooked all the way through? What does it look like?), **so I do these on separate pans** (see previous pan question).

Onion, chopped (one onion?)
Garlic, minced (how much garlic? A whole garlic or a clove?) (what is the difference between minced and chopped?)
Olive oil
Tomatoes, chopped (use canned tomatoes in winter) (how many cans?)
Fresh basil (how much?)

Sauté onion and garlic in olive oil until softened and fragrant (in a frying pan?). **Stir in tomatoes and cook until thickened. Toss in roasted vegetables. Sprinkle with basil.**

I have attached two pictures of ratatouille to this email. Please tell me which one your recipe looks like.

"Jesus, look at this," I said to Blair as I finished reading and turned my computer his way. And although I was growing irritated, we both laughed at how it totally captured the

Badley we knew. I had other things to do, like my job, but I took a few minutes to respond:

> This is not supposed to be complicated. You can use one or 1,000 of the vegetables. How much onion and garlic depends on how much other stuff you have. Let's just say you're doing ½ eggplant and one small of the other vegetables...then about ½ an onion and one or two garlic cloves and a small can of tomatoes should work. Enough oil to lightly coat everything...err on the side of more, it's a south of France dish, it's supposed to be olive oily. Taste the eggplant...it should be tender and luscious, not firm. The eggplant should be lightly golden brown. Use cookie sheets for the roasted veg, a frying pan to sauté the onion and garlic, one large enough to hold all the vegetables. You can serve hot or room temp. I don't have a picture. You should use your common sense or look at a French cookbook for exact measurements...THIS IS A VERY SIMPLE RECIPE.

And he replied:

> As you know there has been no indication throughout my life that I possess common sense in regard to cooking. Do I need to buy a casserole dish to serve this in?

By now, I was reaching the edge:

> Badley, you can just serve it on plates, you really cannot screw this up.

He texted me a picture of his efforts the next day, an array of appetizing color in a white casserole dish, and he mentioned the background check I'd participated in. "I can't believe you didn't know my hobbies. It was hanging out with you, Darlene!" And then he explained the urgency of the recipe:

The reason I had to make Monica dinner was because Nick and Jesse came to DC for the last two weeks and we acted like it was Greek Week. She was not pleased, so I made this meal to make up for it.

And he included another picture, this time of him and Nick and Jesse all smiles at a bar with the caption FRAT FORT-NIGHT.

Not long afterward, Phil and I sat in the bar of RN74 for happy hour before a reservation at the Seattle Art Museum for the Gauguin exhibit. Our server, a smiling and poised young woman in a tight black dress, sat down across from us to explain the wine specials. She transposed the red and white varietals before charmingly correcting herself with "welcome to Friday," and then returned with our glasses and our Ahi Tuna Poppers and Falafel Bites. We had just begun to eat when she returned and again sat down on the adjacent leather ottoman, this time as if she were joining us for cocktails, introducing herself as Nina. "I just realized who you are!" she cried. "I thought I recognized you. You're Darlene!" Which of course I knew, but I wondered how *she* knew.

"I was an Alpha Phi," she went on, referring to the house just across Forty-Seventh Avenue from the Alpha Sig House, "from pledge class '06." It was the year I had started and I thought about what little I knew about that sorority, the times I'd heard seductive singing drifting across the street during the first weeks of school, and the time my guys had reported that the white-coated chefs had served them corn dogs for dinner. "I knew Eliab and Nate and all those guys," she went on breathlessly. "And we used to sneak in and eat your food. And one time I saw you there and wanted to say hi, but you were gone before I could, and we felt guilty, but Nate told us that you hated waste, so it was okay." She told me all of this as if she were in confession as I sat rapt, more than happy to forgive all. I realized that she was older than the food bandits I knew about and that the sorority food-theft capers had begun in my first weeks on the job. More important, those memories of real food had stayed with her and made her so happy that she wanted me to know.

In May, the University of Washington chapter of Alpha Sigma Phi celebrated its hundredth year, so the usual Founders' Day celebration continued into the weekend and drew brothers from all over the country, including the national office in Indiana. Bob seized the opportunity to hit up the more wealthy alumni with a precelebration lunch, charging them hundreds of dollars for the privilege of an invitation to what was supposed to be an exclusive meal at the House, prepared by me. But the interior condition of the place was such that he decided they were all more likely to open their wallets for the swanky Hotel Deca a few blocks away. A more inclusive reception followed at the House, where $50 secured admission to an open bar, tended by sorority girls in dresses that made me want to stand behind them when they reached down into ice chests for more liquor, and to a buffet catered by someone else, freeing me up for conversation as well as butt coverage.

As always, Founders' Day coincided with Greek Preview, the annual neighborhood tour for graduating high school seniors and their parents. So while other houses were quiet for the weekend, the visitors could see a ripping party going on at the Alpha Sig House, complete with an obviously large and dedicated group of alumni. Usually this was a positive thing, since active membership participation was a sign of a healthy House bank account and continued growth and vibrancy of the fraternity. But this particular year the level of celebration was such that it was more startling than attractive to many of the parents streaming by. And when it came time for a group picture, the entire pledge class of 2002 was on the roof, barely able to balance while singing "The Table's Set":

Drink, drink, drink to our fraternity,
Drink, drink, drink for she means so much to me.
Good fellowship is forming here, so may it never die!
Drink, drink, drink to Alpha Sigma Phi.

And just when I was feeling like it was well past time for me to go, Tony and Josh, who'd been seniors when I was hired and were now practicing attorneys, came over to hug me and talk about the early days. As we stood there laughing hard about their previous cook and my rough adjustment and my crazy obsessiveness before they finally taught me to take myself less seriously, the current freshmen looked over at us, as if wondering who those people were, and why they knew me, and I suddenly felt very rooted here, as rooted as any of them.

Richard returned from his studies in Belgium the week after Founders' Day, making the kitchen his first stop and me the first person to give him a hug and a welcome home. He'd posted pictures of his time abroad and had seemed to be on a perpetual spring break, touring and beer sampling and rafting on the Rhine while we slogged through Seattle's dreary winter. But everyone in the House was overjoyed at the news that he was back. "You are so loved here," I told him after watching the fifteenth person light up and ask for a hug upon sight of him. I thought at times that it would be nice to be so universally popular, but that would require being emotionally temperate, unfailingly kind, judicious, thoughtful, nonjudgmental, relentlessly upbeat, and motivating. "God, the guy's annoying," I remarked to Blair as I laughed that I was never going to be that person and as he simultaneously observed that he was himself the opposite of each of those descriptors.

But Blair had his own strengths, and in the summer he headed for a coveted internship with Safeway's corporate office in California, where Corey was in law school. The two of them cooked together, texting me pictures of their efforts with messages like, "Some food porn for you . . . perfectly crispy, perfectly 165° chicken thighs," and "Disregard the curly fries, but you should be proud of our Jalapeño Cheddar Stuffed Turkey Burgers with Grilled Cactus Leaves. We miss your cooking!!" Richard remained in Seattle and cooked as well, living in the House over the summer and sending me his own pictures. He added to the first one that "we aren't all hopeless individuals," without elaborating on who the hopeless were.

Like most of the seniors, Blair and Richard would be moving out in the fall, making room in the House for twenty-five new pledges. I couldn't know exactly what was ahead, but I knew it was a different landscape in many ways. John sent me a list of new products his company would be selling, a range of organic and non–genetically modified items and an entire line of chef-created prepared foods with ingredients I could find in my own pantry. There'd be a presidential election, the second since I started, and new elections in the House, subtly changing the character of the fraternity for the year, with new officers determining the relative emphasis put on grades or philanthropy or, as had been Badley's focus, fun. But there was one thing that I was fairly certain would be constant and I shared it with my husband, Phil, over dinner one night when I was having my usual summer doubts about returning and was explaining what always sent me back. "Everything in my life could be falling apart, I could feel like a worthless failure, and I could show up at the House and there would be only one thing they would say to me: 'What's for dinner?'" And I knew that's all I'd need to hear to know that it really was going to be fine.

ACKNOWLEDGMENTS

No one achieves anything alone, and at no time has that been more apparent to me than while I wrote this book.

So thanks first to my guys, the men of Alpha Sigma Phi, Mu Chapter, University of Washington, who were not just material for this book, but material that formed the last few years of my life. And thanks also . . .

To my husband, Phil, for encouraging me to write about my work in a blog years before there was a book deal and for cheerleading me through the many hours of toil to meet deadlines that always seemed to collide with our plans. I will always remember sitting in our hotel room on spring break in Barcelona working on Chapter Eight while you slept in nearby, so I can't read those pages without thinking of tapas and Gaudi and your unfailing belief in me.

To my sales reps from U.S. Foods, Rod, John, and Kirk, who put up with my sometimes atrocious behavior (which they so diplomatically called "passion") in pursuit of the best, made me laugh at myself, and continued to take my calls and call me a friend.

To my late father, who modeled a profound work ethic, integrity, and appreciation for food that is the foundation of this book, and to my mother, who instilled in me a sense of what it is to be both a strong woman and a caregiver. And to my brothers and grandparents and sons, who are the backstory of this work.

To my agent, Christy Fletcher, who never wavered in her support, slogging through those first drafts and calling this "The Book," even at times when I could not see it as anything more than a big mess.

And to everyone at Hyperion who had a hand in this, especially my editor, Elisabeth Dyssegaard, who gently and skillfully guided me to turn the mess into a published work.